Everyday
Gita

Sunita Pant Bansal started writing poems and stories at the age of eight and has not stopped since. She practised as a nutritionist for a couple of years before deciding to follow her passion. In her four decades of writing career, she founded a weekend newspaper and three magazines, and edited five; she also wrote numerous articles and produced a short film.

Sunita hails from the Kumaon hills of the Himalayas, a region well-known for its crop of littérateur. She started exploring mythology and its impact on our culture. Her forte is decoding Hindu scriptures to show their relevance and application in today's times. She has authored hundreds of books for children and young adults on folk literature and mythology. For adults, her genres cover body, mind and soul, with her books being sold in multiple languages globally.

Everyday *Gita*

365 Days of Wisdom

Sunita Pant Bansal

RUPA

Published by
Rupa Publications India Pvt. Ltd 2022
7/16, Ansari Road, Daryaganj
New Delhi 110002

Sales centres:
Bengaluru Chennai
Hyderabad Jaipur Kathmandu
Kolkata Mumbai Prayagraj

Copyright © Sunita Pant Bansal 2022

The views and opinions expressed in this book are the author's own and the facts are as reported by her which have been verified to the extent possible, and the publishers are not in any way liable for the same.

All rights reserved.
No part of this publication may be reproduced, transmitted, or stored in a retrieval system, in any form or by any means, electronic, mechanical, photocopying, recording or otherwise, without the prior permission of the publisher.

P-ISBN: 978-93-5520-263-5
E-ISBN: 978-93-5520-271-0

Twelfth impression 2024

15 14 13 12

The moral right of the author has been asserted.

Printed in India

This book is sold subject to the condition that it shall not, by way of trade or otherwise, be lent, resold, hired out, or otherwise circulated, without the publisher's prior consent, in any form of binding or cover other than that in which it is published.

*To my Dadaji, who gave me my first Gita,
and to Sunil, my brother, who epitomizes the Gita*

Contents

Preface	ix
The Bhagavad Gita in a Nutshell	xi
1. Arjun's Dilemma	1
2. Transcendental Knowledge	2
3. Path of Karma Yoga	32
4. Path of Gyana Yoga	54
5. Path of Renunciation	68
6. Path of Meditation	86
7. Knowledge of the Ultimate Truth	108
8. Attainment of Salvation	121
9. Secret of Supreme Knowledge	135
10. Manifestation of the Absolute	151
11. Vision of the Cosmic Form of Krishna	157
12. Path of Bhakti Yoga	162
13. Creation and the Creator	173
14. Three Qualities of Material Nature	188
15. Realization of the Ultimate Truth	197
16. Divine and the Demonic Natures	205
17. Threefold Faith	210
18. Final Revelation of the Ultimate Truth	225
Acknowledgments	255

Preface

Bhagavad Gita is the universal truth, it is the song of the Spirit. It gives us knowledge of the Self and answers two universal questions: 'Who am I?' and 'How can I lead a happy and peaceful life?'

On the first day of the great war of Mahabharata, Arjun, one of the Pandavas, faced a major dilemma. He had to make a choice between fighting the war and killing his teachers, friends and relatives or running away from the battlefield for the sake of avoiding violence and preserving peace. He wanted to do the latter.

The 700 verses through which Krishna, Arjun's charioteer, relayed practical wisdom to him is known as the Bhagavad Gita. At the end, a confident and decisive Arjun went on to fight and ultimately win the war.

Arjun's dilemma was, in reality, the universal dilemma. All of us face dilemmas, big and small, in our everyday life while performing our duties. For instance, there is always a tug-of-war between our workplace and family responsibilities. At the core of every dilemma stands our mind and intellect facing each other. The impulsive tendencies (Kauravas) of our blind mind (Dhritarashtra) and the self-disciplined thoughts (Pandavas) of our intellect (Pandu) fight a battle every day with our body being the battlefield (Kurukshetra).

Krishna suggests through the Bhagavad Gita that we should indulge in a daily honest introspection to see which force, good or evil, wins the daily battle everyday.

I have grown up seeing my grandfather and father maintaining daily diaries. During our moral education classes in school, we were asked to remember God every night at bedtime and apologize for any mistakes done during the day. Daily introspection has been a part of my life and the genesis of this book.

Since it's a daily battle we fight, I condensed the seven hundred verses of the Gita to fit into the 365 days of a calendar. I have simplified the verses and explained their essence, drawing from my life's experiences. The purpose is to read one verse a day, understand it and mull over it—I promise it will help you understand the world better.

I have spread out the 17 chapters (Ch 2–18) of the Gita over 12 months or 365 days and given a brief synopsis of each chapter in 'Bhagavad Gita in a Nutshell' in the beginning of the book itself, as a ready reckoner.

This book is an attempt to initiate the reader into the rhythm of the song of the Spirit, demystifying life and its illusions.

Sunita Pant Bansal

The Bhagavad Gita in a Nutshell

To obtain liberation from the cycle of rebirths is the main theme of the Bhagavad Gita, for which it advocates three spiritual paths, namely karma yoga, gyana yoga and bhakti yoga.

The first chapter is about 'Arjun's Dilemma'. It introduces the circumstances and the characters involved. The scene is the battlefield of Kurukshetra; the main characters are Krishna and Arjun. Arjun is struggling with his inability to fight and kill his friends and relatives on the battlefield; he is unable to understand or justify the dharma or logic behind his actions.

Chapter 2 is about 'Transcendental Knowledge.' Becoming his student, Arjun requests Krishna to teach him how to get rid of his sorrow and confusion. This chapter is often seen as a summary of the entire Bhagavad Gita itself as it describes the importance of the immortal nature of the soul existing within all living beings.

Chapter 3 is the 'Path of karma Yoga'. Krishna explains the duties of humans as members of society, and the reasons and benefits related to those duties. The theory of actions leading to bondage is explained.

Chapter 4 is the 'Path of Gyana Yoga'. Krishna reveals how the supreme knowledge is the culmination of the paths of karma and gyana yoga. He also explains the nature and purpose of his descent (avatar) into the material world, which is to establish order by transforming the wicked whenever there is a rise of evil in the world.

Chapter 5 is the 'Path of Renunciation.' Krishna explains the concepts of action with detachment and renunciation of fruits of actions, and that both paths are a means to the same goal of salvation. A yogi or a renunciate is defined as one who finds happiness with the Self, who rejoices in the Self within and who is illuminated by the Self. Such a yogi becomes one with the universal energy.

Chapter 6 is the 'Path of Meditation.' Krishna reveals the nature of the mind and teaches yogic techniques and meditation. The mastery of the mind is the key to liberation.

Chapter 7 is the 'Knowledge of the Ultimate Truth.' Krishna imparts knowledge of the absolute reality and the way to understand it. He describes the illusory material world, how it deludes the mind and the difficulties encountered in clearing the latter.

Chapter 8 is about the 'Attainment of Salvation.' Krishna emphasizes on the knowledge of yoga, the importance of the very last thought at the time of death. The creation of the material and spiritual world as well as the distinction between the two are explained well; the light and dark paths of leaving this material existence, the destination to which they lead to and the reward received through embarking on each path are also described. The path of light (of spiritual practice of yoga and meditation) and the path of darkness (of materialism and ignorance) are the two eternal paths chosen by mankind. The former leads to liberation and the latter leads to rebirth.

Chapter 9 reveals the 'Secret of Supreme Knowledge.' Krishna explains how the entire material existence is created, maintained and annihilated by his will and energy. Devotional service and surrendering to the Lord is seen as a sure path to liberation.

Chapter 10 explains the 'Manifestation of the Absolute.' Krishna presents himself as the cause of all causes, specifying his manifestations.

Chapter 11 shows the 'Vision of the Cosmic Form of Krishna' to Arjun.

Chapter 12 is the 'Path of Bhakti Yoga.' According to Krishna, the steadfast devotee, who is ever content, has controlled his senses, has a firm resolve and whose mind is engaged in devotional practices, is the best of yogis.

Chapter 13 describes the 'Creation and the Creator.' Krishna reveals the distinction between the physical body and the immortal soul, as that between the perishable and the eternal. One who is able to understand the difference between the cause of creation (creator) and the effect (what is created) becomes liberated. One who understands the difference between the creation (body) and the creator (universal energy) and knows the technique of liberation (of individual soul) from the trap of the material world with the knowledge of the Self, attains the Supreme.

Chapter 14 describes the 'Three Qualities of Material nature.' The three modes, namely *sattva*, *rajas* and *tamas*, modes are explained, along with how they influence every aspect of the life of an individual; the chapter also explains that liberation cannot be achieved without transcending these three modes.

Chapter 15 deals with the 'Realization of the Ultimate Truth', where Krishna reveals his transcendental nature and how this applies to everything that exists. He describes himself as being Supreme in relation to both transcendent and immanent levels of existence. Thus, Krishna appears to be omnipotent, omniscient and omnipresent for both manifest and non-manifest reality.

Chapter 16 defines the 'Divine and the Demonic natures'. Krishna describes the divine properties as well as the conduct and actions that are righteous by their nature and conducive to dharma. Ill conduct and its sinful actions are also defined. The knowledge of the scriptures is recommended in order to follow the right conduct.

Chapter 17 is the 'Threefold Faith'. Krishna classifies the three divisions of faith and their links to the three modes of nature. The three divisions of faith are known as sattvic, rajasic and tamasic—these are seen as determining one's consciousness in this world.

The eighteenth or the last chapter is the 'Final Revelation of the Ultimate Truth'. Krishna concludes and emphasizes on karma yoga as the path of performing actions in the world with the idea of offering everything to the Lord.

By the end of this discourse in the Bhagavad Gita, Arjun finally attains the understanding of liberation and liberation itself by performing his duty as a warrior in the battlefield of Kurukshetra.

1

Arjun's Dilemma

In ancient India, there was a king who had two sons, Dhritarashtra and Pandu. The former was born blind, therefore, Pandu inherited the kingdom. Pandu had five sons who were called the Pandavas. Dhritrashtra had 100 sons, called the Kauravas. Duryodhan and Yudhishthir were the eldest of the Kauravas and the Pandavas, respectively.

After the death of King Pandu, Yudhishthir was to rightfully become the king. However, Duryodhan, being jealous, planned several schemes to kill the Pandavas and take away their entire kingdom. He succeeded in doing so unlawfully and refused to return even an inch of the land without a war.

The war of Mahabharata was thus inevitable. The Pandavas were unwilling participants. They had only two choices: fight for their right as a matter of duty or run away from the war and accept defeat in the name of peace and non-violence.

Arjun, one of the five Pandavas, faced this dilemma while standing in the battlefield, leading his army. He had to choose between

(a) fighting the war and killing his revered teachers, dear friends, close relatives and many innocent warriors or
(b) running away from the battlefield for the sake of avoiding violence and preserving peace.

That's when Krishna, his charioteer, gave him a discourse of 700 verses, what is known as the Bhagavad Gita. Simultaneously, this discourse was also narrated to King Dhritarashtra, by his charioteer Sanjay, whie giving an eyewitness report.

2

Transcendental Knowledge

1 January–11 February

JANUARY

Day 1

You grieve for those who are not worthy of grief, and yet speak words of wisdom. The wise grieve neither for the living, nor for the dead. (2.11)

Some people talk one way and live another; there are a few who truly walk the talk. There should be consistency in what we say and what we genuinely feel.

People speak very sensibly about life and its trials, yet when they are faced with situations like missing the bus or a flight, they immediately become stressed. This is where one must do some introspection and remove this two-facedness. The wise do not waste their time in complaining or crying over things that are changeable. Better time management can help prevent instances of missing a bus or flight.

Those who complain and get distressed are the ones who believe in the sense of possession and expectation. It is a myopic way of looking at the world. Death of a loved one reminds us that it is God's world and nothing belongs to us; we cannot possess anything or anyone and when there are no possessions, how can there be any expectations?

One may look at the ocean and see the rise or birth and fall or death of the waves on the surface. One may see the indivisibility or oneness of the entire mass of water in its depths. The wise only see the indivisible mass of water. They understand that little pebbles do not cause commotion in the entire ocean.

Day 2

There was never a time when these monarchs, you, or I did not exist, nor shall we ever cease to exist in the future. (2.12)

Change is the only constant. In this world, there is a constant change in form and expression, but the essence within these changes remains.

See the water cycle; water from the Earth's surface evaporates and rises up to form clouds, which then get heavy and release the same water back on the Earth as rain. The trees shed their dead leaves every autumn, forming the soil in which fresh seeds grow to form new trees. Life dies to nurture new life.

The human soul also keeps dying and keeps taking birth. The soul is the non-physical essence of a living being. After death, it gets another life in a new and different form. This is the philosophy of reincarnation.

The new form that the soul takes is the expression of desires that it carries over from its previous life. All its present desires would, likewise, find expression through a different body in the future. This play of cause and effect of desires, resulting in different bodily forms or births, goes on indefinitely, according to Krishna.

Day 3

Just as the embodied soul acquires a childhood body, a youthful body and an old body during this life, similarly, the soul acquires another body after death. This does not bother the wise. (2.13)

We live many lives in one lifespan. As a small child, a youth and then as an old person, our physical, mental and emotional experiences are very different; these life stages are almost like individual and independent lives. The clock keeps ticking.

But every time, it is the body that goes through changes, the soul remains the same. It is the soul, the consciousness that looks back at the past with nostalgia and looks forward to the future with excitement. Once the body gets too old and weak to handle the soul, it leaves that body and finds another. There is still no change in the soul. And this happens with all living beings.

Since our own body cannot be expected to live forever, how can we expect others to be there for us forever? It is wise to not expect anything to provide us with everlasting happiness, be it our family, friends or material possessions.

When we leave our school or university, we leave behind most of our friends. When we move to another city to work, we leave behind our neighbours. Life goes on. Material objects also become meaningless after some time, when we are too old to appreciate them. The wise realize the temporariness of everything and form no attachments.

Day 4

The contact of the senses with the sense objects gives rise to the feelings of heat and cold, pain and pleasure. They are transitory and impermanent. Therefore, one should learn to endure them patiently. (2.14)

Our sense organs are very sensitive and respond pleasurably or painfully to stimuli. They have been conditioned to have strong likes or dislikes.

There is no reaction when ice touches a stone, but when it touches the human skin, there is a definite sensory reaction. The human brain recognizes the perception of ice as cold. It is conditioned to interpret that sensation as pleasurable or disagreeable, depending on the person.

It is simple—I may like the sensation of cold, you may not.

The interpretation of any perception as good or bad is dependent on the preconditioning of the brain, and the body is accordingly directed to react. The coldness of skin is superficial, but the perception is mental. A chloroformed person, for instance, is unable to perceive any sensation even if you put ice on their skin.

Interestingly, continuous contact with any stimulus results in acclimatization. We get used to it. So, after a while, we do not feel good or bad. Since our senses are bound to encounter all sorts of stimuli, it is up to us to condition our mind to be less affected (or unaffected) by them. Such a non-excitable state of mind gives immense peace.

Day 5

A calm person, who is not affected by the sense objects and is even-minded in pain and pleasure, becomes fit to attain everlasting happiness. (2.15)

The feelings of pain and pleasure have a common source, desire. Fulfilled desire is pleasure and unfulfilled desire is pain. And desire is produced through contact with the objects of the senses. Both, attachment to pleasure and aversion to pain, disturb the peace and equilibrium of our mind.

I want to buy a pair of blue walking shoes. I go to the market but I am unable to get the right blue or if I do, I'm unable to get my size. There are two options in front of me. I can get all worked up and disappointed and decide to visit the market some other day. I am bound to feel upset till I get the shoes. The second option would be to think what is more important—the colour blue or the shoes? If my brain is not worked up, I will either buy the shoes in another colour or place an order for my size in blue in the shop where they had the colour but not my size.

We must see for ourselves and realize how our feelings and

our reactions bind us to our body and its environment. Only if we become neutral in our reactions can we get out of this bondage.

A changeable mind gets easily disturbed. The mind which is in a constant state of unruffled peace despite all kinds of sensory experiences gains everlasting happiness.

Day 6

The invisible soul is eternal and the visible physical body is transitory. The reality of these two is indeed known to men of wisdom. (2.16)

The ocean can exist without the waves but the waves cannot exist without the ocean. The ocean is real and the waves are transitory. Whenever there is a storm, the essence of the ocean remains the same; it's the waves that change in form and nature. And these waves can carry a person away from reality.

We are in the grip of our senses and get carried away by the material world around us. The glitz and glamour fuel our desires and we spend our waking time struggling to satisfy them. We are surrounded by temptations and are controlled by the media; we are told it is okay to get loans to satisfy our larger-than-life desires. We do not realize that it is a bottomless pit.

Trapped in the manifest material world, we forget that we have to leave all this behind when we die. The ordinary person considers the materialistic world as real because it manifests and the soul as unreal as it is hidden. Such ignorance is the cause of all suffering—the suffering of running after the acquisition of material goods and then the fear of losing them.

The wise see through the veil of delusion and recognize the impermanence of the outer material world. They recognize and appreciate the inner soul and, hence, remain forever happy.

Day 7

The Spirit by whom this entire universe is pervaded is indestructible. No one can destroy the imperishable Spirit. The physical bodies of the eternal, immutable and incomprehensible Spirit are perishable. Therefore, fight! (2.17–2.18)

When an earthquake destroys a house, the clay remains. It's the same with water that turns into ice or steam. Its form may change but the essence remains the same. The air we breathe cannot be seen but can be captured in balloon and watched as it floats.

In the same way, the Spirit or the energy, which some call the universal soul or God and which pervades everything in this universe, remains hidden and is indestructible.

The body will ultimately grow old and die. So it is best to fight the senses and destroy the attachment to this mortal body. As, sooner or later, the immortal soul is compelled to leave the old mortal body and find a new one as its next abode.

Our senses are constantly creating traps for us to strengthen our attachment to our body. We want to dress it better, beautify it with artificial means, feed it with harmful foods and drinks—in short, we are lost in a self-created sensual world.

The wise are never lost. They fight their senses and keep them under control. They do not form an attachment with their mortal body but enjoy the freedom of their soul.

Day 8

The one who thinks that the soul is a slayer and the one who thinks the soul is slain, both are ignorant. Because the soul neither slays, nor can be slain. (2.19)

Since the soul is immortal and indestructible, it naturally means that it cannot be destroyed. And since it is omnipresent, pervading everything, it cannot destroy anything for it cannot destroy its own self. Scientists have also proved that energy can neither be created, nor destroyed. It only gets re-arranged.

This does not mean that we kill someone on the premise that we are not killing the soul, but just killing the physical body. The law enforcers would certainly not be amused with this logic!

The action of killing would bring its own results, by way of getting punished by the law of the land. Apart from that, the feeling leading to such an action would attach and enmesh the soul more firmly in the seemingly unending cycles of births and deaths.

At the end of the day, anger or any other emotion that makes us act a certain way is also a form of bondage. We are allowing our emotions to control us; the wise do not do so, they understand the imperishable nature of the soul and, thus, are at peace.

Day 9

The soul is neither born, nor does it die at any time. It does not come into being or cease to exist. It is unborn, eternal, permanent and primeval. The soul is not destroyed when the body is destroyed. (2.20)

The universal Spirit or primal energy is reflected in all living things, just as the moon is reflected in water. It is like the reflection of the moon in a bowl of water; once the bowl is broken, the reflection disappears. But the moon remains where it was. If we get another bowl of water, the moon's reflection would be seen in that. So the bowls may change, but neither does the moon change, nor does its reflection.

In the same way, the universal Spirit reflects in us as our soul. The soul is not destroyed when the body is. The various stages of life—birth, existence, development, change, decay and death—also do not affect the universal Spirit or the soul. When one mortal body is destroyed, the soul gets reflected in another.

As the nature of the moon and its reflection do not change, the universal Spirit and soul also are unchangeable. As the moon's reflection is not attached to the changeable bowl of water, the soul too is not attached to the changeable mortal body. The wise understand this and develop detachment from their physical bodies.

Day 10

How can a person who knows that the soul is indestructible, eternal, unborn and immutable, kill anyone or cause anyone to be killed? (2.21)

If we realize that the same universal Spirit inhabits everyone, and that we all are the same at the spiritual level, then we would hesitate to hurt or kill anyone. This is a reasonable thought of a reasonable person. But many a times, situations become such that a perfectly reasonable person suddenly becomes unreasonable.

If a vicious person attacks a virtuous one and their family in order to rob them, the latter is likely to put up a fight. By law, it might be wrong if the vicious person gets hurt or killed in the fight; the virtuous person's actions, however, would be not be wrong morally.

It's similar to soldiers fighting on the battlefront. They certainly do not like killing people, but have to do it as it is the question of killing their enemies. We need to always see the larger picture.

For self-defence or for the sake of justice, if our actions hurt others, we should not let that bog us down or change our path. We need to detach ourselves from emotions and carry on doing the right thing. Humans are pawns in this game of life. The wise person understands this and rises above any emotional attachment to the activities of this illusory world.

Day 11

Just as a person puts on new garments after discarding the old ones, similarly, the living entity or the individual soul acquires a new body after casting away the old body. (2.22)

It is normal for humans to change clothes daily, the same way it is normal for the soul to change physical bodies. Just like an actor may play many roles in a play on stage, by changing costumes, a soul also plays many roles in this drama of life by changing bodies.

It is easier to get new clothes if one is willing to discard the worn-out ones. Similarly, it is less painful for the soul to move on if one is unattached to the mortal body. Some people are extremely attached to their bodies, death scares them. But the wise welcome death because they know they would be entering a new body.

In our lifetime, we are full of wishes that we are always striving to fulfil. When our body becomes old and infirm, we still do not want to pause. We continue wanting more. Death comes when it has to and when it does, we take our residual desires with us to the next life. The cycle of karma goes on till we no longer hold any desire and ends with us no longer coming back in another body. This is the theory of reincarnation or rebirth.

Day 12

Weapons do not cut the soul, fire does not burn it, water does not make it wet and the wind does not make it dry. The soul is eternal, all pervading, unchanging, immovable and primal. (2.23–2.24)

A soul is a fine vibrational form or reflection of the universal Spirit or the supreme energy. It is primal, omnipresent and indestructible by water, wind, fire or weapons.

In order to create any impact, the energies should match, like a solid breaking another solid; but the solid cannot break liquid or gas. So, how can the soul be destroyed? There is nothing that matches the supreme energy!

The entire creation is an illusion, like a dream or a drama. The universal Spirit is the dreamer of this dream. There might be a calamity in our dreams, but we continue to dream, unaffected. The flood and fire of the dreams do not hurt us and we wake up safe. Likewise, the universal Spirit, the dreamer of the creation, is unaffected by any mishap to the creation.

The mortal body suffers but the soul residing in it remains untouched. After the suffering is over, the body gets destroyed and the soul is free. The universal Spirit wakes up from the dreaming state, safe and unaffected, to create yet another illusory body for the soul that was freed. The dream goes on.

Day 13

The universal Spirit is said to be unexplainable, incomprehensible and unchanging. Knowing this, you should not grieve for the body. (2.25)

Before the creation was created, before the dreams were dreamt, the universal Spirit was present. Then the different body forms were dreamt into existence, with the Spirit reflecting in them as their souls. The forms changed, but the reflection remained the same.

It is like when we watch a film in a theatre. A film is nothing but a bunch of moving characters that come alive on the blank screen in front of us. Looking behind us, we can see the beam of light coming out from the projection room and falling on the screen in front. Similarly, the illusory world is the film created by the Spirit.

Every character on the screen seems real, till the projection beam is switched off. Once that happens, the characters created by it also go away. But we don't grieve for them; we know it was just a film.

There is no universe without the universal Spirit. It's the Spirit that creates the ever-changing universe, while itself remaining the same. The wise understand the true changeless nature of the Spirit and do not grieve when their loved ones leave. They know their souls will return in new bodies.

Day 14

Even if you think that the physical body takes birth and dies perpetually, even then, you should not grieve. Because death is certain for the one who is born, and birth is certain for the one who dies. Therefore, you should not lament over the inevitable. (2.26–2.27)

According to the law of cause and effect, the soul is destined to change its mortal residences. Once the soul has been caught in the web of delusion or maya, it has to go through a series of prisons of mortal births and deaths to fulfil its desires and pay for the debts incurred by its own actions or karma.

Every desire is logged in as karma, even if we do not act on it physically. As we grow up, our desires seem to increase steadily. The more we see things around us, the more we desire to have them. These desires create a web around us, from which there is no escape.

Since each action or karma has a reaction, we cannot escape the cycle of cause and effect. So it is senseless to complain about the operation of the universal law as we have no control over it.

A better proposition would be to consciously reduce our desires. Fulfilling our desires for material things gives us momentary happiness, whereas freedom from all desires gives us permanent happiness.

Day 15

All beings are invisible to our physical eyes before birth and after death. They manifest between the birth and the death only. What is there to grieve about? (2.28)

Just because air cannot be seen does not mean that it is not there. We know it is there all around us; we are breathing it.

We don't always have to see the source of things, nor do we have to worry about where things go to in the end. As we switch on the television, we see the images that entertain us. The images disappear when we switch off the television. So, does it matter where they came from and where they went? What should matter is that we enjoy the programme that we are watching.

We need to learn to be mindful of the present and be happy. The past is gone and the future is yet to come; it's the present that is alive.

Can we do anything about what has happened in the past? Can we turn the clock back? Do we know what is going to happen tomorrow? What we certainly know is today, the present. We should not grieve what we don't know about. Let us live in the present and enjoy every moment of it.

Day 16

The Spirit that dwells in the body of all beings is eternally indestructible. Therefore, you should not mourn for anybody. (2.30)

When we mourn somebody's death, we actually mourn for ourselves. This may seem odd, but it is a fact, that we mourn a relationship that we have lost, a loss of a comforter and an emotional partner.

The body alone dies, not the soul. And if we understand the indestructible nature of the soul then we would not mourn. We would then understand that the soul has left the body to find a new and better one. We would say that so-and-so has left this world or passed on, rather than saying so-and-so is dead.

Love for the person should not be limited to their body; it should be for the soul inside that body. That way, when the body dies, the love remains because the memories of that soul would continue to live forever.

Day 17

Considering your duty as a warrior you should not waver like this. Because there is nothing more fortunate for a warrior than a righteous war. (2.31)

We all have roles to play and duties to perform in society, for it to exist and grow. The monarchs or the leaders have to govern, the warriors have to fight the enemies, the farmers have to grow food, the teachers have to teach and the labourers have to labour.

A society or a country can function smoothly only if all perform their duties well. Likewise, in a family too, the members perform their respective roles of being a breadwinner or homemaker to maintain a balanced family life.

At a micro level, all the organs in our body, including the sense organs, have their individual functions to perform. If any one of the organs fails to perform or lags behind in performance, an imbalance is caused and the body falls sick. The role of our mind (head) here is to monitor the rest of the organs. This is the genesis of the phrase, 'head' of the family.

At the level of our individual selves, the mental (spiritual) warrior in us should fight the momentary sensual attachments to protect our kingdom of mental peace.

Day 18

If you will not fight this righteous war, then you will fail in your duty, lose your reputation and incur sin. (2.33)

It would be wrong to refuse the opportunity to fight and conquer the enemies that are threatening our welfare. It's like refusing to take medicines for a disease we are suffering from.

When we find ourselves in a situation whereby our mental peace is threatened by sensual temptations, we should fight to conquer them. If we don't fight to gain self-control, then we would end up being sense-controlled. A self-controlled person is governed by wisdom, whereas the sense-controlled are slaves of their senses. This would eventually lead to misery and sickness. The classic examples of sense-controlled people would be addicts and gamblers, though those would be extreme cases.

In the larger perspective too, whether in a family, society or country, the roles and duties are distributed according to the capabilities of people. If anyone fails, it inevitably results in chaos.

A righteous war is that which is supported by our wisdom, where our conscience is clear. If we fail to be righteous, sooner or later, our conscience will prick us. That sense of guilt, of not having done the right thing, will haunt us till death.

Day 19

You will go to heaven if killed in the line of duty or you will enjoy the kingdom on earth if victorious. Therefore, get up with a determination to fight. (2.37)

Life is a battle that all of us have to fight, facing our individual problems. Those who fight and solve their problems are naturally happy with their success. But those who fight and yet do not succeed are not complete failures either, as they grow in strength.

Valiant losers are not cowards. People who are victims of greed, anger, gluttony and other such sensual vices and are trying to overcome them should not give up in the face of failure. They have to continue trying as they would surely be successful one day. They are heading towards it one step at a time.

However restless we may be, because of our habits and an environment full of temptations, we can still fight our way out of inertia with our determination. Patients suffering from a terminal disease continue to try all possible treatments available to them. Death is inevitable, but at least they die satisfied that they left no stone unturned.

Day 20

Treating pleasure and pain, gain and loss, victory and defeat alike, engage yourself in your duty. By doing your duty this way, you will not incur sin. (2.38)

The basic principle of yoga is to practise mental equilibrium to neutralize delusion. This does not mean automation, but discrimination and self-control. Control here means control of emotions like attachment or repulsion, longing or unwillingness—these extreme emotions cause us to lose our balance, like a pendulum swinging wildly. A calm and balanced mind alone can take wise decisions. The middle path is the right path.

The people who are overjoyed by their temporary success seldom achieve permanent prosperity. Their success becomes their distraction. The resultant overconfidence may lead them to take high risks and wrong steps towards an eventual failure.

Likewise, disillusionment and depression after a failure also make people lose their focus. It impairs their ability to renew their efforts, thus reducing chances of any success in future.

The wise remain unruffled in any situation they face. Their minds are balanced like a tractor, unaffected by the ups and downs of the path they follow.

Day 21

No effort is ever lost in selfless service, and there is no adverse effect. Even a little practice of the discipline of selfless service protects one from the great fear of repeated birth and death. (2.40)

Any effort, even if unfinished, is not wasted. In fact, even the mere desire for liberation leads one to it. It's the secret of manifestation. We desire something and, armed with faith and positive thoughts, we set out to achieve it. More often than not, we are successful.

The desire for peace, however fleeting, takes root in the subconscious and eventually bears fruit when the appropriate time comes.

If we start the process of keeping our senses under control, we will eventually manage to do so. And the result will be everlasting peace.

Just as a step in the right direction leads us towards freedom from the karmic cycle, material pursuits would always lead us to all kinds of traps. It is up to us to choose the path before taking the first step.

Day 22

A selfless worker has resolute determination for God-realization, but the desires of the one who works to enjoy the fruits of work are endless. (2.41)

For any task to be successfully executed, it is important to be focused on it. It is like aiming at the bull's eye when you shoot. Multitasking is never successful, but setting goals and prioritizing them is.

When we set our target in a work environment, we direct all our energies and resources towards achieving it. We end up successful. If we have a direction and a goal, we would reach it, but if we go in multiple directions, we would never reach any goal and would end up being thoroughly confused.

It is the same with life. The temptations are endless. They do not allow us to achieve our goal, enmeshing us in a web of desires. Considering that not every desire can be fulfilled, our life can never be happy or content; we would always be facing disappointments. Focussed journey leads us to peace, whereas directionless journey creates an endless karmic cycle of births and deaths.

Day 23

You have control over doing your respective duty only, but no control or claim over the results. The fruits of work should not be your motive and you should never be inactive. (2.47)

Some people live only for their own selfish happiness. They are attached to the results and work as the sole beneficiaries of their actions. Such self-centred people get continuously led from one desire to another. Ultimately when their end comes, they realize that all their wealth would be left behind for others to use. Such people always live their lives dreading their end.

This is not to say that we should lack ambitions or targets in life. We should have goals to achieve, wealth being one of them. The problem comes when we get so lost in acquiring wealth that we forget everything and everyone else. Even if we manage to make some people happy with our wealth, we still would be leaving it all behind when we die. Isn't it better that we use some of our wealth to help those in need?

When we die, we leave behind memories. People whom we have helped in their times of need remember us forever. Whereas those who are not needy, to whom we have given our wealth, do not appreciate our gift. A person who has five pairs of shoes is unlikely to be grateful on receiving another pair. At the same time, one who doesn't possess shoes would be forever grateful when they are gifted a pair.

Attachment to the fruit of the action should not be the driving force. Attachment makes us unreasonable. However, non-attachment to the fruits of action should not make you inactive. Action is important, regardless of whether it fetches you the desired result or not. Attachment is not great as it creates bondage.

Day 24

Do your duty to the best of your ability, abandoning worry and selfish attachment to the results and remaining calm in both success and failure. Selfless service is a yogic practice that brings peace and equanimity of mind. (2.48)

The word yoga or yogic practice signifies the mental evenness that is the result of communion of the mind with the universal Spirit. Mental evenness is the natural state of the soul. Earthly material attachments disturb this evenness or balance of the mind. A chaotic mind results in a chaotic life.

A person of attachment always reaps unhappiness. Their worldly minds become uneven by gains and losses, wins and defeats. The unattached person, whereas, remains undisturbed and forever in peace.

The key is to do any and every task with devotion, commitment and honesty towards the task, not its result. In this way, we do not get attached to the result, be it good or bad. Where there is no attachment there is no disappointment and, hence, no chaos or imbalance of the mind.

Day 25

Work done with selfish motives is inferior to selfless service. Therefore, be a selfless worker. Those who work only to enjoy the fruits of their labour are always unhappy because one has no control over the results. (2.49)

It is foolish to work for personal gain as it gathers only troubles through ever-increasing desires. The results of such actions are uncertain and transitory. It can be seen all around us.

People work towards earning more money to buy bigger houses, bigger vehicles, more clothes, more jewellery, more gadgets, basically to acquire more and more material goods. Very soon, these things go out of date and the urge to acquire more continues. All marketing is aimed at fanning our desires and greed. The result of this kind of selfish action always results in stress and misery.

It is wise to work selflessly, unaffected by temptations. The result would be peace and happiness. Once we understand the basic nature of the universal Spirit that pervades all of us and the fact that all the wealth that we accrue stays back when we die, it becomes easier to not form attachment to that wealth.

Day 26

Working to the best of one's abilities without becoming selfishly attached to the fruits of work is called karma yoga. Karma yogis are freed from the bondage of rebirth due to renouncing the selfish attachment to the fruits of all work, and they attain the blissful divine state of salvation or Nirvana. Therefore, strive for selfless service. (2.50–2.51)

Prisoners who serve their term rebelliously stay in the prison till the end of their term. Those who serve their term with good conduct please their warden and may be let off before their time.

Similarly, when we lead our life rebelliously, going in and out of desires, we ultimately get stuck in them. Since desires are never-ending, we still carry them in us when we die. Our soul then has to take birth again to fulfil those leftover desires. The karmic cycle of birth and death goes on.

To carry on with life's activities absolutely selflessly, without any attachments, is karma yoga or the art of proper action. And it frees the soul totally from the earthly bondage of karmic effects of actions.

The soul of a selfless person changes from a body-identified, limited and karma-bound entity to a state that is ever free and beyond the influence of karma. So a person, by performing all actions with the conscious awareness of the universal Spirit or God, remains in peace and happiness forever.

Day 27

When one is completely free from all desires of the mind and is satisfied and happy with the universal Spirit, then one is called an enlightened person. (2.55)

The wise know that their inner self is the universal Spirit that contains all the bliss. They know that the same Spirit is in everyone. When everyone is the same, then where is the need to discriminate or compare? When there is no comparison, there would not be any competition or petty jealousies among people.

Once we start shedding our desires, we start feeling free. After all, it's the desires that bind us down. We buy something good and then we spend more time in looking after it and worrying for its safety. It is the same with the smallest to the largest material object.

Without desires, there wouldn't be any attachment, even if we possess precious things. Hence, we wouldn't worry about their safety.

Shedding desires goes a long way in making us peaceful. Having such steady wisdom is called getting enlightened.

Day 28

A person whose mind is unperturbed by sorrow, who does not crave pleasures and who is completely free from attachment, fear and anger, is called an enlightened sage of steady intellect. (2.56)

The wise person or an enlightened one remains beyond the reach of common emotions. They do not become inwardly perturbed or bothered or stressed when in trouble or when things don't go their way. They also do not get unduly elated or excited over their success.

Why? This is because a wise person has neither attachments, nor desires. Desire, when unfulfilled, gives rise to emotions like fear, anger and disappointment. The same is true for any attachment; it gives rise to fear of loss.

People of steady intellect, who are not shaken by the drama of the world around them, are enlightened indeed. Such people are very successful in life as they can continue to forge ahead in their profession without getting affected by their environment.

Day 29

The mind and intellect of that person become steady, who is not attached to anything, who is neither elated by getting desired results, nor perturbed by undesired results. (2.57)

People who can perceive the separateness between their soul and the excitable nature of their body and mind, remaining unaffected by the pleasures and pains of their body, have unwavering wisdom.

Such people are often called heartless or cold-blooded or indifferent by their friends and family. This is not so. Being calm and balanced in every situation is being neutral, not indifferent. It requires conscious effort to control the ever-excitable senses. It needs wisdom to understand the fickle nature of the material world.

Such people have realized that God or the universal Spirit is within them. They are aware that the soul is ever at peace, even when the body is ceaselessly experiencing the dualities of pleasure and pain. Such a person is like God and deserves respect.

Day 30

When one can completely withdraw the senses from the sense objects as a tortoise withdraws its limbs into the shell for protection from calamity, then the intellect of such a person is considered steady. (2.58)

The tortoise swiftly withdraws its limbs into its shell when faced with any danger. Similarly, we withdraw our five senses into our subconscious mind during sleep or deep meditation.

But then, we also have the capacity to withdraw our senses

while awake, if we so want. When we are told that a certain type of food, say sugar or gluten, is bad for our health, we are able to withdraw our craving for it and avoid it altogether. Likewise, we can control the cravings of all five senses if we decide to do so or if we are convinced that doing so would help us lead a better, healthier and happier life.

People who have consciously attained this freedom from sensory intrusion, the ones who can voluntarily withdraw their mind and energy from any of the five senses, are the true yogis.

Day 31

The desire for sensual pleasures fades away if one abstains from sense enjoyment, but the craving for sense enjoyment remains in a very subtle form. This subtle craving also completely disappears for the one who knows and understands the universal Spirit. (2.59)

Physical self-control without mental self-control is of no use. A person may distance themselves from sensory temptations but their minds would constantly be dwelling on it, and may sooner or later succumb to it.

It is like fasting, an imposition that we know will end soon and we eagerly look forward to that end. Doesn't the mind think more about food while fasting? Such abstinence is only superficial; the mind is not abstaining.

Running away to a hermitage or a retreat is escaping from reality. If we want to get away from the clutches of our senses, we need to exert mental control. Physical abstinence is incomplete without mental abstinence. Having understood the presence of the universal Spirit within, the wise have no interest in sensory pleasures.

FEBRUARY

Day 1

Restless senses forcibly carry away the mind of even a wise person striving for perfection. (2.60)

The wise, while trying to overcome the sensory stimulations, should not only stay away from the temptations externally, but also control their senses internally.

Our subconscious is very powerful and feeds the senses with the images of the past sensual experiences. In moments of weakness, we can fall prey to temptations.

It is like building the immunity of our physical body. We work hard to take precautions to make our body immune to infections. But unknown to us, germs are present inside us at all times. The germs start flourishing the moment our immunity drops.

Thus, we should introspect periodically to find out if we have been successful in controlling our desires or are they just hiding for the time being.

Day 2

One should fix one's mind on the universal Spirit with loving contemplation after bringing the senses under control. One's intellect becomes steady when one's senses are under complete control. (2.61)

The victim of self-indulgence would not have a steady intellect and would always have clouded judgment, moving on from one error to another.

Our senses are so powerful that they control us without even letting us know about it. A glimpse, a whiff, a faint sound or a memory can trigger an avalanche of desires in us. Our desires keep pushing us in multiple directions, leaving us confused and directionless in the end.

The wise should withdraw their minds from their senses and keep it united with the universal Spirit. Such outer and inner control makes the intellect steady. This does not happen overnight; it has to be practised consciously and regularly so that it becomes a habit. We can consciously train our subconscious to keep our senses in check.

Once achieved, steady wisdom helps us to exercise the right judgment in all our decisions and actions.

Day 3

One develops attachment to sense objects by thinking about sense objects. Desire for sense objects comes from attachment to sense objects and anger comes from unfulfilled desires. (2.62)

Attachments can happen any time. Seeing something beautiful can result in a desire to possess it. In fact, visualizing any kind of sensory happiness produces an attachment to that feeling of happiness. Such attachment develops into a desire. And we know that the objects of desire are many; they could be people, pets, gadgets, property, food, clothes, jewels—anything at all.

Once the desire enters our system, our mind gets focussed on fulfilling it. We think of ways and means to possess our object of desire. If, unfortunately, we do not succeed, then the same unfulfilled desire, which was earlier the cause of anticipatory happiness, becomes a cause of anger.

If the desire is righteous, the resultant anger would also be righteous and it would result in applying extraordinary efforts to pursue it. But if the anger is egotistical, then the results can be very damaging.

Unrighteous anger make people lose their balance of mind. Such a person may implode with heart attack or stroke or explode and become aggressive. Most crimes are triggered by anger resulting from unfulfilled desires.

Sense attractions should, therefore, be sublimated right in the beginning before they get the chance to grow into desires.

Day 4

Delusion or wild ideas arise from anger. The mind is bewildered by delusion. Reasoning is destroyed when the mind is bewildered. One falls away from the right path when reasoning is destroyed. (2.63)

Non-fulfilment of desires agitates the calmness of the mind, arousing wrath and resulting in blinding confusion or delusion. This delusion stupefies the mind and dulls its reasoning power.

Loss of memory follows delusion—memory of their own dignity, their real nature, of what they are supposed to do. Such a person is unable to distinguish between right and wrong. Without the ability to distinguish, the path leads to destruction and misery.

Road rage is a classic example of this. We start a day well, looking forward to a fruitful meeting at work or we end the day tired, looking forward to a quiet dinner with family—in either case, we are driving. Suddenly, another vehicle overtakes us from the wrong side so fast that it brushes against our vehicle. Our vehicle gets a nasty dent. Meanwhile, the culprit seems unapologetic, oblivious of breaking the traffic rule.

Such an incident always gives rise to anger. If we allow that anger to grow, it would result in us getting out of our vehicle to shout at the offender. Or else, we lose our cool and jump a traffic light. There could be any number of consequences, and might even lead to an accident. Our day gets ruined effectively.

Day 5

A disciplined person, enjoying sense objects with senses that are under control and free from attachments and aversions, attains tranquillity. (2.64)

If there is an attraction, there is a corresponding aversion. We love the taste of sweets and get attracted to any and every dessert. With such a sweet tooth, it's highly unlikely that we would be attracted to anything bitter; in fact, we would be averse to bitter foods.

Our attractions and aversions, likes and dislikes, are at the root of our entanglement in the material world. They make us a slave to moods and habits.

Self-controlled people, armed with wisdom and non-attachment, perform their duties happily in the world full of temptations, confident of their success at all times. Such wise people are like swans swimming in muddy waters and yet not getting their wings dirty.

Day 6

All sorrows are destroyed upon attainment of tranquillity. The intellect of such a tranquil person soon becomes completely steady and united with the universal Spirit. (2.65)

The secret behind the success of all online portals that are selling goods and services is the vulnerability of our senses. These portals pamper our senses with attractive visuals and convince us that we must buy, or even just try out, their products. More often than not we succumb to these temptations.

Why? Because we are governed by our senses and are under their control, whereas, it should be the other way round—we should be controlling our senses. We should have the wisdom to decide what we need. Uncontrolled desires create chaos in life.

Self-controlled people are unaffected by any temptation and hence lead a peaceful life. They understand the true nature of the universal Spirit and the material world. They know that the material world cannot provide everlasting peace or happiness. This wisdom not only guides them but also guards them against all temptations.

Such people are balanced in thought and deed and do well

in their professions too. Only a balanced mind can take the right decision at the right time.

Day 7

There is neither Self-knowledge, nor Self-perception in those who are not united with the universal Spirit. Without Self-perception there is no peace and, without peace, there can be no happiness. (2.66)

If one is not in light, then one is in darkness. Opposites co-exist like night and day. It is said that unless we go through sadness, we are unable to appreciate happiness. So, this vacillation from one to the other continues throughout life. Accordingly, our mind also reacts to the situation at hand; it also vacillates.

When we keep getting pulled by our senses, how can our mind maintain its balance? Those who are attached to the senses are, therefore, never in balance. They are obviously not connected with the soul, as the soul is eternally peaceful. A person in tune with their soul would be unruffled and peaceful in all situations.

Peace does not mean indifference; many a times people develop indifference to the material world after they've been through some tragedy. That peace is negative. Positive peace results from Self-knowledge and wisdom.

The mind is like water—you can't see a thing if it's turbulent but if it's calm, you can see everything. The calmness of mind comes from understanding the truth about our soul and the universal Spirit reflecting in it.

Day 8

The mind, when controlled by the roving senses, steals away the intellect from the spiritual shore of peace and happiness, just as a storm takes away a boat on the sea from its destination. (2.67)

In good weather, on a calm sea, a boat can sail easily and reach the shore. But the same boat would be thrown off course in a storm.

Our intellect is like a boat. Our mind is like the sea. Our senses create a storm in that sea through our various attachments. How can a person possibly succeed in distinguishing right from wrong when caught up in a storm of attachments?

The sensory temptations overwhelm and confuse us. We get distracted and diverted from our natural course of good intentions.

It does not mean that we cannot get back on the right path. We still can. We just need to still the storms of our senses. Humans are born good; it's the sensory distractions of the material world that trap them and change their lives. Running after peace and happiness is actually us running away from those. But hope is not lost. Once we get our control back in our hands, peace and happiness come to us naturally.

Day 9

Those people whose senses are completely withdrawn from the sense objects are the ones whose intellect becomes steady. (2.68)

Our wisdom is the charioteer controlling the sense horses that carry us to eternal peace and happiness, riding through a terrain of sensory temptations.

A person without self-control is unable to prevent the horses from running wild in multiple directions in pursuit of sensory pleasures. On the other hand, a wise person is able to guide the horses firmly towards the path of virtue.

At the same time, it is not advised to tie up the sense horses. That is not real control; training the horses to be obedient is the real way of controlling them. Removing a person's eyes does not destroy their desire for sensuous beauty. The senses cannot act by themselves; they direct the mind to generate action. Hence, it is important to free the mind from the enslavement of the senses.

A wise person's chariot would always be steady, as it would be driven by controlled horses. Leaders are effective only when their decisions are taken by their intellect and not by their emotions.

Day 10

One attains peace, within whose mind all desires dissipate without creating any mental disturbance, as river waters enter the full ocean without creating any disturbance. One who desires material objects is never peaceful. (2.70)

Even though many rivers flow into it, the ocean remains ever unchanging and ever full. Peaceful people are somewhat like that. The souls of peaceful people are the oceans of contentment in which their entire consciousness is immersed. They absorb within themselves all the desires and yet keep overflowing with energy, contentment and peace.

Ordinary people are not completely at peace. Their level of peace is like a tank of water that is bombarded continuously by many little desires that surround them. These desires bore holes in the tank, from which the water starts trickling out. Soon those people lose their peace completely.

Instead of losing their peace through small yearnings, human beings could learn to control their desires. Another way is to help others in need and spread happiness. It is paradoxically true that our joy increases when we help others, but decreases when we are pursuing our selfish desires.

Day 11

One who abandons all desires, and becomes free from longing and the feeling of 'I' and 'my', attains peace. (2.71)

Peace is a product of freedom from all desires. It may not always be practical as there are certain obligations that we have for our own health, our family and our work. But then, we can still avoid getting entangled in the jungle of material objects.

More than that, we need to take the tough call of freeing ourselves from the inner longings for the objects we have relinquished. Our inner desires cause more bondage, and hence more damage, than the material temptations of the world.

True renunciation does not necessarily mean leaving the material world and going to the Himalayas to live in a hermitage. Renunciation is dropping all attachments, dropping the concept of 'mine'. As with everything else, renunciation is also in our mind.

Once we are able to renounce the world in our minds, we do not need to go anywhere. We can continue living our normal life and it would be peaceful and happy. Freedom from ego and its earthly attachments results in everlasting peace.

3

Path of Karma Yoga

12 February–13 March

Day 12

In this world, there is a twofold path of spiritual discipline. The path of Self-knowledge for the contemplative ones, and the path of selfless work for all others. (3.03)

The way of wisdom and the way of right action are the two paths to attain eternal peace. The way of knowledge and discrimination, known as gyana yoga, is for the wise. The way of right action, known as karma yoga, is for all the others.

The wise study the scriptures to understand the real nature of soul and the universal Spirit. But mere theoretical wisdom is not enough. The scriptural knowledge has to be applied in life to experience its spiritual precepts.

Studying and acquiring degrees is great, but those degrees don't help us get food on our plate or a roof on our head unless we use them to get a job. We need to apply our education in practical life for it to bear any fruit.

Likewise, right action alone is of no use, unless it is selfless in nature. People get attached to their philanthropic activities and want to be recognized for it. They promote themselves as the messiah for the needy. Aren't they missing the whole point? Right action means selfless action, an action with no hidden agenda or attachment.

Most of the so-called philanthropists are obsessively attached to their actions.

The two paths of gyana and karma yoga merge in the end. Wisdom and selfless work together lead towards eternal peace.

Day 13

One does not attain freedom from the bondage of karma by merely abstaining from work. No one attains perfection by merely giving up work because no one can remain action-less even for a moment. Everyone is driven to action by the forces of nature. (3.04–3.05)

Freedom from karmic bondage does not come from renunciation of work. Work alone does not create karmic bondage, our thoughts and desires do so too. So there can be no absolute action-less moment. We are either restlessly active or actively restless.

Though wisdom is considered superior to activity, ultimate knowledge cannot be attained without climbing the ladder of social, moral, religious and meditative activities. Wisdom is not served to us on a platter; we have to work towards acquiring it. When we are thrown into the river of life, we need to swim to save ourselves and move ahead.

The entire cosmos is created and guided by the interplay of three qualities or modes of expression, sattva (elevating), rajas (activating) and tamas (obstructing). So, as an integral part of the vibrating cosmos, human beings are compelled to perform some or the other action. The trick is to be detached from the fruits of all actions. By doing so, the wise person is forever calmly active and actively calm.

Day 14

Anyone who restrains the senses but mentally dwells upon the sense objects is called a pretender. (3.06)

The people who subdue their senses outwardly, becoming recluses, but still think about the objects they have forsaken, are merely deluding themselves. It's like people fasting. Many people fast for religious reasons and it's a task for them; they would avoid going out for fear of temptation or gorge on food the night before.

Dieting is similar. People who follow strict restricted diet to lose weight gain it back almost immediately once they stop dieting. Why? This is because they have forced themselves to fast or diet; they are not mentally convinced or committed to it. The moment they are allowed to, they eat and they eat more to compensate for the earlier abstinence.

The thoughts and deeds should be in harmony because if the inner temptation increases to flood-like proportions, then the outer self-control may be swept away.

Control of action should always begin with control of mind. In order to overcome a temptation, it is important to convince the mind, giving reasons for abandoning the thought and, hence, the action.

Day 15

The one who controls the senses by the trained and purified mind and intellect, and engages the organs of action to selfless service, is considered superior. (3.07)

People who keep their senses under control, remaining unattached to their own desires and ambitions, will ultimately manage to follow the righteous path. That path will lead them to eternal peace and happiness.

Keeping our senses under control requires practice, which we would do only if we understand the benefit of self-control.

Going back to the example of dieting, if we understand the basics of nutrition and know what each food is doing to our body, then it would be easier for us to follow the right diet. This wisdom comes from knowledge, and that guides our actions.

The wise control their senses and direct their organs of activity on to the path of right action. Such selfless activity is karma yoga.

Day 16

Perform your obligatory duty because working is indeed better than sitting idle. Even the maintenance of your body would not be possible without work. (3.08)

The universal Spirit that permeates every cell of cosmos is at peace, yet is actively performing all functions to maintain life.

Nature all around us, including the plants, animals and the people, is growing constantly, non-stop. The growth doesn't stop even if there is a natural calamity like earthquake, typhoon, etc. Even our body doesn't stop growing even for a second, does it?

Humans are in the image of the universal Spirit. They are also expected to be actively performing all their duties related to the maintenance of their body and life. It's a simple enough task, but since we are endowed with a thinking brain, a mind of our own as the phrase goes, we tend to get swayed by our senses.

If wisdom prevails, our mind controls the sensory horses and leads us on the right path and in the right direction. If it's the other way round, then the horses lead us wherever they want to go.

Doing nothing is not the solution. In fact, idleness is a crime of sorts, as we all have our duty towards our creator and society. Even the one who has renounced the material world, has a spiritual responsibility of setting an example to the world.

Day 17

Work, other than that done as a selfless service, binds human beings. Therefore, becoming free from selfish attachment to the fruits of work, do your duty efficiently as a service to me. (3.09)

People who work for selfish motives like material profits and happiness are doomed to be karmically tied to the earth through many incarnations.

If we pause and introspect, we would find that whatever work we do has a selfish reason attached to it. It may start small as a means to provide for ourselves and our family, but then it goes on to buying a bigger place to live, a bigger vehicle to drive, expensive clothing, holidays abroad, sending children to expensive schools and so on—the list grows.

Our definition of providing for our family and ourselves changes over the years. Unknown to us, our greed, our attachments, increase. We start changing jobs to increase our salaries, so that we can buy more. Decades ago people would stick to a job, but not now. Now, if you meet someone after five years, you'd find them doing a different job than before, and perhaps looking for yet another change.

These are bondages that we are getting trapped into; nobody is happy. If we work without getting attached to its fruit, we would be saved from all this stress. If we stop running after what is there in the market, we would find contentment with what we have. That is the path to eternal peace.

Day 18

In the beginning, the creator created human beings together with selfless service (yagya) and said—by serving each other you shall prosper and the selfless service shall fulfil all your desires. (3.10)

All human beings are created from one source, the universal Spirit or cosmic intelligence. All are given divine wisdom.

The word yagya means that we do something and get something back in return. People in the ancient times did yagyas propitiating gods to get a son or a particular superpower. Their wishes were granted depending on the intensity of the doer's devotion or commitment. The yagya was like a cow that would be milked whenever the need arose.

Yagya is equated here to selfless service. It is selfless service that gets us what we really want. The word 'really' is the key. What do we really want? No, not material goods, but eternal peace and happiness.

Humans are endowed with wisdom, which has the potential to guide them in the right direction. Listening to this inner guidance, the wise serve others in selfless service and enjoy peace and happiness forever.

Day 19

Nourish the celestial controllers with selfless service, and they will nourish you. Thus, nourishing one another, you shall attain the supreme goal. (3.11)

In ancient times, people worshipped nature to acknowledge human beings' dependence on the natural forces. They prayed to the sun, moon, rain and various plants. It was a gesture of gratitude as well as a request for maintenance of nature's bounty. Somewhere down the line, humans got so embroiled in their senses that they forgot all about nature. Global warming is the result of the same.

At a micro level, humans are a miniature of the universe in which they live. If they don't look after their own bodies, the bodies will cease to function normally.

Every activity is like a yagya, wherein we give and get. What we sow, so shall we reap, is something we have been taught since kindergarten. But blinded by our greed for satisfying our senses at the cost of others, we move on to the path of self-destruction. All diseases caused by lifestyle are a result of that.

The wise stop running and take charge of their senses. It enables them to move smoothly, unfettered, on to the path leading to eternal peace and happiness.

Day 20

The celestial controllers, served by selfless service, will give you all desired objects. One who enjoys the gift of celestial controllers without sharing with others is, indeed, a thief. (3.12)

We should be grateful to the universal Spirit that makes this body function, and should accept the bounties of nature humbly. Those who do not do so, and feel that all that they are getting is rightfully theirs, are no better than thieves. This applies at all levels.

In nature, we have seen the havoc caused by deforestation and mining. Mostly, these are done by people who own large areas of land. Greed makes them blind and they feel that since they own the land, they can do whatever they want with it. They forget that the forests provide food and shelter to animals and birds. They don't want to share the trees; they would rather cut them and sell the timber. The same is true for the miners who mine indiscriminately. Such people are thieves, stealing from nature.

There are some people who hoard food grains in the hope of selling it at a higher price during shortage. They do this while people in another part of the country are starving. This is also stealing. No one should have to go hungry in the world.

Since we are not learning to share nature's bounty, it is lashing back with calamities like floods, famines, tsunamis, and of course, global warming.

Day 21

The righteous who eat after feeding others are freed from all sins, but the impious who cook food only for themselves, without first offering to God, or sharing with others, verily eat sin. (3.13)

The fundamental principle of yagya should be applied to life at all times. We should give first before getting anything. That giving may not necessarily be actual physical giving, but can be symbolic by way of gratitude.

For instance, before eating any meal, we should feel grateful for what we have on our plate. When we are young and dependent, we should be grateful to our parents or whosoever is providing for us.

All through our lives, the feeling of gratitude should remain alive in us. Not only does it ground us, it actually makes us understand the value of every little thing in life.

Those who are oblivious of and thankless to the source or the giver remain within the karmic cycle of rebirths. The universal Spirit balances out everything, so when we just take and take, we have to come back in another life to give back.

Day 22

From food, creatures spring forth; from rain, food is begotten. From the sacrificial cosmic fire, rain issues forth; the cosmic fire or light is born of karma or divine vibratory action. This divine vibratory activity comes to being from God's creative consciousness; and this consciousness is derived from the everlasting universal Spirit. (3.14–3.15)

Food is the fountain, the sustainer of life, and water is the sustainer of food. Water comes from the cosmic fire, the cosmic light. And this cosmic light comes from the universal energy.

Hence, the cosmic energy of the creative cosmic vibration is the source of all life and life-sustaining food. This is the law of creation. Humans are also a product of cosmic energy, of the life current that condenses as earth or matter or food.

This is to understand that at the atomic level, everything that we see around us has the same source. We come from the same source and get absorbed back into the same, when our time ends.

Nothing is superior or inferior; everything is the same bunch of atoms but clustered together differently. It is indeed a humbling thought. It's like a huge mass of Lego pieces that are joined together in different ways to create different objects. Understanding this reality of the universal Spirit, the wise remain unaffected by the sensory world.

Day 23

The one who does not help to keep the wheel of creation in motion by selfless work, and rejoices in sense pleasures, that sinful person lives in vain. (3.16)

According to Hindu scriptures, this is not the only life that we have; we have lived before and will live yet again. We need to accept the present and take responsibility of the future.

This understanding helps us to appreciate the ever-changing world around us. Being a part of this ever-changing world we should fulfil our duty towards it. We should actively look after nature and our environment as we draw our sustenance from it.

People who are wrapped up in their own selves, in satisfying their sensual needs, end up being restless and unhappy, as all the senses can never be fully satisfied. Such a person is born and dies without leaving any impact on anyone. What a waste!

Day 24

The one who rejoices in the soul, who is delighted with the soul, and who is content with the soul alone, for such a self-realized person there is no duty. Such a person has no interest, whatsoever, in what is done or what is not done. A self-realized person does not depend on anybody for anything, except on the universal soul or God. (3.17–3.18)

When we are conscious of our physical body, how we look and pander to the demands of our senses, we get lost in 'I, me and mine'. This is ego. Ego has a tendency to grow very fast. People who are lost in their ego have no time left for anything or anyone else.

Such people impose their ego on their family as well. They want to be seen in designer clothes and luxurious cars. They even put pressure on their children to do certain courses or follow certain professions to maintain their image.

Humans are endowed with imagination, which can be very troublesome at times. Egotistical people always live in their imagination. They constantly look for validation from people around them.

On the other hand, the wise live within their soul, in the blissful understanding that everything gets left behind when the soul moves on to the next body. Such people are not attached to their body, nor dependent on anyone; they are self-controlled and at peace with themselves and the world.

Day 25

Always perform your duty efficiently and without any selfish attachment to the results, because by doing work without attachment one attains eternal peace. (3.19)

When we do anything, we always have a reason for it. Doing a job or business, for instance, is done to earn money for sustenance. Initially, it is self-sustenance, but subsequently, the requirement increases as the family grows. So, attachment to result of work is understandable.

The key word here is 'selfish'. When a normal straightforward justifiable attachment becomes selfish, we don't get to know. It starts with fulfilling the basic needs, and then greed enters the picture. Over time, we start earning more; when the needs have already been satisfied, vanity takes over. We start pampering our senses with rich food, beautiful accessories, expensive perfumes, visit to theatres and other such luxuries.

With this, we have crossed over to the zone of 'selfish'. In this zone, no amount of wealth is enough, as the senses are insatiable. The wise know how to not fall into this trap. They keep a control over their senses. Since they don't develop any attachments, they don't suffer from any disappointments. They are at peace, forever.

Day 26

King Janak and others attained perfection of self-realization by selfless service (karma-yoga) alone. You should also perform your duty with a view to guide people, and for the welfare of society. (3.20)

It is not necessary to ignore our household or family duties and pursue charity or selfless work. King Janak, for example, was a great and noble king, who efficiently performed his duties towards his kingdom, yet remained unattached to it all. His people considered him to be a saint.

Another example would be Mahatma Gandhi. He was a well-educated man from a well-to-do family who could have practiced law successfully as he was a trained barrister. But he was not attached to the sensory material world and decided to help the people of India to attain freedom from British rule. That was selfless service.

The point being emphasized here is that selfless service is doable. Any person, who decides to help others, sharing his knowledge or wealth with those in need, is on the right path.

Day 27

Because whatever noble persons do, others follow. Whatever standards they set the world follows. (3.21)

Ordinary people have a herd mentality. They look around for leaders to follow; it saves them from thinking.

So, if we genuinely want to help others, we should set an example for them. We should follow the path of selfless service with full commitment. People around us would tend to emulate and follow us. This is how goodness spreads. And if, because of us, people start changing for the better, it would be a tremendous achievement.

One thing to remember here would be that we should not get attached to the thought of people following us. We should just do what's right for us to do, without looking back, and continue doing so till the end of our lives.

At the micro level, this means that our senses behave according to what our mind feels. If the mind has anger, the senses also reflect the same—music will seem like noise then. If the mind has bliss, the senses will reflect the same—one would be tolerant to others' mistakes.

Day 28

As the ignorant work with attachment to the fruits of work, so the wise should work without attachment for the welfare of society. (3.25)

When we do gardening as a hobby, we enjoy seeing the fruits of our labour in the form of colourful flowers. The sight is pleasing to others too and it's great for the environment.

But, when hired gardeners do the same gardening, they are not as pleased with their work. They are just doing their job, and their worry is that the owner of the garden should be pleased. All the efforts that they put in gardening are to please their employers enough to raise their salary. The same gardening does different things to different people because the perspective varies.

When we do something as a hobby, we are not attached to the fruit of the action; we are doing it for the experience, the feeling of happiness that we get out of it. When we do something as a job, we are attached to the fruits of our action. That causes expectations, resulting in stress.

Isn't it better then, to do everything as a hobby, so that we get pleasure doing it? No attachments, no expectations, only peace and happiness!

MARCH

Day 1

The wise should not unsettle the mind of the ignorant ones who are attached to the fruits of work, but the enlightened one should inspire others by performing all jobs efficiently without selfish attachment. (3.26)

It is not possible for all to follow the spiritual path. Everyone has a role to play in this world for it to function. We need our farmers, builders, tailors, teachers, soldiers, bankers, doctors and others. All the jobs are interconnected and have to coexist peacefully.

All of us are born for a reason. And we are entitled to work towards our social and economic growth. But there comes a time in our lives when we are tired of running after material things and the perennially elusive peace. At that time, we should pause and reset our goals. We should start ridding ourselves of our material attachments and start on the path of selfless service.

Each person is different in this world, with different speeds of growth and levels of understanding. Nobody should force their understanding on the other. It is best to follow one's own path and set an example for others to follow.

Day 2

The forces of nature do all the work. But due to delusion of ignorance people assume themselves to be the doer. (3.27)

Nature has three primary components or principles: sattva, the principle of harmony; rajas, the principle of activity; and tamas, the principle of passivity. They are the causes behind the feelings of pleasure, pain and indifference.

These three principles or attributes are present in everything in the world. The nature of anything, be it good, bad or indifferent, is based on the predominance of any of the three principles.

Interestingly, the proportions of these attributes keep changing and they are the cause of all attachments in a person. How? The predominant attribute of the mind acts like a lens that affects our perception and perspective of the world around us.

If the mind is governed by rajas, it perceives the world to be full of activity and reacts to it accordingly. Likewise, if dominated by sattva, it perceives the world to be joyful; if led by tamas, the world seems confusing.

The wise understand this and know that they are not the doer of any activity, it's the nature's forces that create and generate activity.

Day 3

The one who knows the truth about the role of the forces of nature in getting work done does not become attached to the work. Such a person knows that it is the forces of nature that get their work done by using our organs as their instruments. (3.28)

Once we understand the forces of nature playing within us, we can observe them in a detached manner.

A friend gets promoted and we congratulate them. Then, after a while, we start feeling jealous. We question their deservedness and we assume that they must be indulging in sycophancy to get promoted. We think of everything possible that they must be doing other than doing their job well. It does not occur to us that they could be genuinely capable and efficient in their work. This is how jealousy colours our thoughts.

Emotions like jealousy, rage, lust and craving make us do things that we would not in a calm state of mind. In rage we can attack someone, lust results in rapes, craving can make one steal and a jealous person can find devious ways to destroy the other person's achievements.

Since we know this, we can actually be alert to any such emotions entering our mind. We can analyse and understand their cause. Once we become observers of this cause and effect phenomena, it would be easy to detach ourselves from it.

Day 4

But those who are deluded by the illusive power (maya) of nature become attached to the works done by the forces of nature. The wise should not disturb the mind of the ignorant whose knowledge is imperfect. (3.29)

We see all kinds of people around us, but it's not for us to judge them. We only have to observe and help them when they seek help. Everyone has a path, following which they grow and evolve. And that path depends on their intellect and understanding of what they need to do.

A student knows what he/she has to study to become a doctor. Merchants know what goods they have to stock to sell. Cooks know what ingredients they have to buy to cook a certain dish. A teacher knows what to teach. The list is endless.

The point here is that we all know what we are doing and we certainly do not appreciate anyone interfering in our business. Try telling your mother how to cook a dish that she's been cooking for many years. Or try telling the plumber how to fix the leaking tap.

Likewise, every person has an inbuilt system of emotional responses. They have their own levels of attachment to senses. Once they get tired of running after their desires, they pause and wonder. That is the time when they seek help to understand the forces of nature that govern them. That is the time when they start asking questions. And that is the right time for us to help them, not before. It's the patient who has to go to a doctor, it's never the other way round.

Day 5

Do your duty, dedicating all work to God in a spiritual frame of mind free from desire, attachment and mental grief. (3.30)

There is always a reason or a motive behind any action. We need to understand that. The motive could be guided by our past experience or by our future goal.

A child wants to grow up to be a doctor and heal people. It is a very popular dream profession of many children. When the time actually comes to appear for entrance tests to study medicine, the child suddenly recalls how the sight of blood had made them recoil when they had seen their sister cut her hand. Based on that childhood memory, they decide that medicine is not the right profession for them. Do you think they are right?

Similarly, a child is all set to enter medical college and study to become a doctor. Their heart is set on becoming a dermatologist. A friend tells them of an uncle whose practice as a dermatologist turned out to be a flop because of a bunch of skin clinics mushrooming in their neighbourhood. The friend declares that becoming a dermatologist is a waste of time as there is no dearth of people curing skin problems. Should this be an influencing factor for a person to study or not study dermatology?

Thoughts of past or future are always debilitating. We should stay in the present and do what we are doing, without any distractions. This is the only way we would be saved from mental grief. An unattached mind is always at peace.

Day 6

Attachments and aversions for the sense objects remain in the senses. One should not come under the control of these two because they are two major stumbling blocks, indeed, on one's path of Self-realization. (3.34)

Love and hate are the two sides of the same coin, as they say. It is true. When we love someone, we are consumed by that emotion and everything in our life revolves around them. When our loved one breaks our heart, we go to the other extreme—we start hating that person. And again this hate consumes us as we think of ways and means to hurt our ex.

In both scenarios, the emotions ultimately harm us. We are totally controlled by those emotions. The only way out is the middle path of moderation, which happens only if we are not attached to our sense objects. This does not happen overnight. We have to understand why we need to be detached; suppressing attachment is not the solution.

When we are told that sugar is harmful to our health, we stop consuming all forms of sweets. This results in suppression of our desire. One day our resolve breaks and we suddenly gorge on all desserts that are available. The right course of action would be to understand why and how much of sugar is harmful to our body. We can then consume it in moderation.

Likewise, once we understand why attachments and aversions are harmful, we can learn to deal with them effectively.

Day 7

One's inferior natural work is better than superior unnatural work. Death in carrying out one's natural work is useful. Unnatural work produces too much stress. (3.35)

It is natural for parents to want their children to follow their footsteps, their line of work. It may work many a times, but in some cases it doesn't. The child of an industrialist may want to become a musician.

The parents want their child to handle their family business while the child wants to set up his own music studio. The situation is likely to be very volatile. There would be pressure on the child to study in order to join the family business. If the child succumbs, they would be studying under tremendous stress. And where is the guarantee that the child would be as successful as their father after joining the family business? Who is happy in such a situation?

For everyone's happiness, it is advisable to follow what our gut tells us. Following someone else doesn't lead us anywhere. It is better to be doing what satisfies us and makes us happy rather than doing something half-heartedly.

Day 8

It is the desire born out of passion that becomes anger when unfulfilled. Desire is insatiable and is a great devil. Know this as the enemy. (3.37)

Anger management is becoming an industry of sorts. It seems there are more angry than happy people in this world. Why? Anger is the result of unfulfilled desire. And it has a tendency to grow very rapidly, like a virus. Interestingly, happiness doesn't stay for long with us, but anger does; it can actually stay forever.

If children are angry with their parents, they grow up to become angry adults who take out their pent up anger on their subordinates at work. The genesis of road rage is almost always some frustration caused by an unfulfilled desire in the past, which boils over by any trigger on the road. It has nothing to do with the issue at hand.

This is how dangerous suppressed emotions can get. The root cause being the desire, generated by the senses, in response to the material world around us.

If we learn how to not feel disappointed at the first instance of our desire not being fulfilled, we will go a long way in controlling our desires and developing detachment.

Day 9

As a fire is covered by smoke, a mirror by dust and an embryo by the amnion, similarly, Self-knowledge gets covered by different degrees of this insatiable lust, the eternal enemy of the wise. (3.38–3.39)

We are surrounded by temptations of the material world. Everything—be it property, vehicles, clothes, jewellery, cosmetics, shoes, food, furniture or even services like beauty treatments and bank loans—is being offered at our doorstep at attractive prices.

Who wouldn't succumb! And because of that, the problems are getting compounded. People are dazzled by the easy availability of everything and strive to earn more and more to enjoy these luxuries. But then the story doesn't end here. The market gets flooded with yet more temptations, newer luxuries and the story moves on like the never-ending TV soaps.

The more we get trapped in these material luxuries, the further we move away from real happiness. The sensory pleasures can never end; they have to be kept under check. They're like diabetes or asthma that can't be cured but have to be controlled for our overall health.

Day 10

The senses, the mind and the intellect are said to be the abode of desire; these delude a person by veiling Self-knowledge. (3.40)

Every desire of ours stems from one of our five senses. We smell delicious food and we are tempted to eat it; we hear about an exotic place and we want to go there for a holiday; we see an advertisement of the latest car in the market and we want to buy it; we love the feel of a fabric and desire to wear it; we taste a refreshing drink and want to continue drinking it.

It's all a play of senses. They create desires in our mind. The mind itself cannot do much except push our intellect to take action. If the mind convinces the intellect to buy the car, the intellect would then find ways and means to do so. Likewise, for all the other items.

If we are wise, we would not give in to the mind's temptation; instead we would think further about the usability or importance of that item in our life, like, do we really need that car at this time of our life? Isn't our old car good enough? Do we have the means to buy a new car? And so on.

So, it's up to the intellect whether it wants to fall prey to the desire or not. A strong intellect can tell the mind to shut up and the desire would vanish.

Day 11

Therefore, by controlling the senses first, kill this devil of material desire that destroys Self-knowledge and Self-realization. (3.41)

We go to the market with our children, where they see a toy airplane in a store and want it. Considering it's the first time they have asked for something, we agree to buy it.

Then the same thing happens again. This time they want a toy car. Next time they want a football, then a pair of skates and it goes on. Sounds familiar? This is how habits are formed. They will grow up to behave the same way when they desire something. We have not taught them to be reasonable in their demands.

As adults, we can be more careful. We can pause to think and reason with our own minds—do we really need the object of our desire? We will realize that the moment we start thinking, the desire also loses its intensity. Gradually, we would be able to control it and, with that, we would be able to control our senses as well. The tempting sights and smells of the world would not attract our senses any more.

Day 12

The senses are said to be superior to the body, the mind is superior to the senses, the intellect is superior to the mind, transcendental knowledge is superior to the intellect and the Self is superior to transcendental knowledge. (3.42)

The driver of the vehicle is the one who has to be very careful and alert, as he has to know the right way apart from having full knowledge about the vehicle itself. He has to manoeuvre the vehicle through the ups and downs on the road, keeping it under control at all times. One mistake and the vehicle could meet with an accident or veer off the road and fall into a ditch.

So in life, we need our mind to be alert and careful. Absent-mindedness can cause mishaps. The mind is guided by the intellect, so if the mind is absent, the connection between the intellect and the senses would be lost. The senses would go haywire.

The intellect, the mind and the senses are inextricably interconnected and together run the body. The mind, under the guidance of the intellect, handles the senses. It's our intellect that saves us from greed and gluttony. In the work scenario, our intellect stops us from taking rash, emotional decisions. It's the intellectual maturity that makes us an effective leader.

Day 13

Thus, knowing the Self to be superior to the intellect, and controlling the mind by the intellect that is purified by spiritual practices, one must kill this mighty enemy, desire. (3.43)

Earlier in kingdoms, now in corporates, hierarchy is observed and protocol is followed. The human level of consciousness also follows hierarchy of sorts. The physical body is at the lowest level of consciousness; it's very limited. The senses are superior to it; they have a wider range of activity.

The mind is superior and directs the functioning of the senses. Intellect is superior to the mind because of its capacity to distinguish between right and wrong.

Clearly, our intellect is the CEO of our consciousness and is responsible for all our actions, as the CEO of a company is responsible for its performance. It is up to our intellect to protect us from getting distracted by the sensory temptations and falling into the trap of desires.

4

Path of Gyana Yoga

14 March–1 April

Day 14

Though I am eternal, immutable and the Lord of all beings, yet I manifest myself by controlling the material nature using my own divine potential energy (maya). (4.06)

The universal energy is eternal—it is neither created, nor destroyed. It just changes shapes and forms. This is something that science has proved. Humans are also an energy form, as are other living things around us in the material world.

People get so lost in their family name and background or their educational degrees that they start feeling superior to other humans. They don't realize that family name is just that, a name; it cannot define their nature.

Every human is inherently the same, with the same blood and body organs. It has been proved time and again that when a patient needs blood or an organ transplant, the donor could be anyone, as long as there is tissue compatibility between the donor and the recipient.

The CEO of a company as well as the receptionist, both are humans; this understanding goes a long way in how we treat our fellow human beings. Everyone has a role to play in the functioning of an organization, but outside of that, they are on the same level, that of a human.

Day 15

Whenever there is a decline of dharma (righteousness) and a predominance of adharma (unrighteousness), then I manifest myself. I appear from time to time for protecting the good, for transforming the wicked and for establishing world order (dharma). (4.07-08)

Whenever there is serious tension in our lives, we seek help. It could be from a friend, parent or even a counsellor. A similar thing happens at the macro level. When people at large are going through turmoil or stressful times, leaders or spiritual masters appear to lead them out of it.

Since everything is a play of energy, good and bad both, the bad is transformed into good. This happens by the wise men convincing the bad guys that what they're doing is not good for anyone, not even for their own selves. The good guys help the wise men in spreading this awareness.

Similar transformation happens at a micro level in our own selves. We spend a fair chunk of our lives running after material pleasures and keeping up with the Joneses. One day, we feel tired and stop. That's when we realize our own foolishness of pursuing transitory pleasures.

We introspect and our intellect comes into play then. Our intellect shows us where the real happiness lies. It channels our desires towards helping people, catching up with family, doing something good for the neighbourhood or society at large. The restlessness gets transformed into peace.

Day 16

The one who truly understands my transcendental appearance and activities of creation, maintenance and dissolution attains my supreme abode and is not born again after leaving this body. (4.09)

According to Hindu scriptures, we are born again and again to fulfil our leftover desires. We are okay with it, as we are unaware of our previous life and don't care much about the next. But closer home, unknown to us, we are being sucked into the world of man-made material things. Our houses may be overflowing, but our desires are never-ending.

We cut trees to build bigger houses but then have to plant more to avoid soil erosion. If we had not cut the trees in the first place, we wouldn't have had to plant afresh. We fight with our parents to claim our inheritance and, two decades later, our children do the same with us.

Things go wrong at our workplace, we get upset and shout at our subordinate. He/she complains against us to our boss, who fires us. These things can go on and on like a ripple effect, till somebody in the chain decides to stop it by not reacting.

That understanding, that wisdom of not allowing our emotions to ride over us, is the wisdom that leads to eternal peace. And since this wisdom would result in checking our desires, breaking the cycle of rebirth would be an added bonus.

Day 17

Work does not bind me, because I have no desire for the fruits of work. The one who fully understands and practises this truth is also not bound by karma. (4.14)

People who do their work passionately, getting thoroughly involved in and absorbed by it, will produce a masterpiece. There are many obvious examples of such people in the field of art and craft, like Michelangelo, Van Gogh and writers like Rabindranath Tagore and filmmakers like Satyajit Ray and many more.

Even in the field of science we have had people whose sincere dedication gave us the basic conveniences that we enjoy today. All these people were not aiming at the money they stood to make for themselves; they just did what they did best.

A person whose aim is sensual satisfaction gets trapped in the web of senses. This we have seen and experienced. We buy a small vehicle and, a couple of years later, we are tempted to buy a bigger one. The need hasn't increased, greed has. Greed is a bottomless pit, totally insatiable. It continues forever till we consciously apply brakes to it.

The wise are happy and satisfied with what they do; they are focussed on their work and not on the reward. They are aware that if the work is good, they will get what they deserve. To them, work is relevant to their existence, reward is irrelevant.

Day 18

The true nature of action is very difficult to understand. Therefore, one should know the nature of attached action, the nature of detached action and also the nature of forbidden action. (4.17)

Action is defined as the process of doing something to achieve an aim. So by this definition, talking also is an action and so is keeping quiet, depending on the situation.

Actions are also categorized as good or bad. But then, what is good for some could be bad for another. It's always a matter of perspective. Many times, doctors have to amputate a part of the sick person's body, like a gangrenous limb or a cancerous growth in the intestine. It has to be done to save the rest of the body from the disease.

As long as the reason behind the action is for the larger good, the action is deemed good. If the action is completely selfless, it's termed as detached action. An action carried out for purely selfish reasons is considered as an attached action. Any action that is liable to cause harm in the long run is bad, even though it may seem to be good on the surface; it would be termed as forbidden action.

Day 19

The one who sees inaction in action and action in inaction is a wise person. Such a person is a yogi and has accomplished everything. (4.18)

In a workplace, the higher people go in hierarchy, the lesser they work physically. Their role has more to do with using their brain, strategizing and leading. Are they not working then? Their physical inaction is a more powerful action than the physically active people working under them.

Executives of sales or marketing run around actively to promote their company's product and secure business. But if they do this action without planning a strategy, they will be stuck in making cold calls, without achieving much. In the eyes of their boss, they haven't worked, as work should generate result.

So, we see that action or inaction do not follow a conventional black and white meaning. They are in a grey area and their meaning changes from the perspective of the person looking at them.

At a micro level, when we are pursuing material wealth, our mind continues telling us that we haven't achieved anything yet. It's like we are doing spot running without reaching anywhere.

When we are detached from the sensual pleasures, accruing material wealth has no meaning for us. We use our resources to help the needy. We reach the hearts of many, garnering much love and respect from them. It's like riding an escalator, reaching places without moving.

Day 20

The one who has abandoned selfish attachment to the fruits of work and remains ever content and dependent on no one but God, such a person, though engaged in activity, does nothing at all and incurs no karmic reaction. (4.20)

There are some people who quietly do their job, working through the ranks, and reach great heights in their workplace.

If observed carefully, it will be seen that these people do not get involved in petty politics of the workplace and neither do they hanker after increments and promotions. They simply work to the best of their ability, with utmost sincerity. Since such people do not cause any harm to anyone, nobody troubles them.

Life is also something like that. If we live in harmony with nature and people around us, we will be at peace. If we let go of our sensual desires and attachment to material things, we will be at peace. If we let go of our expectations from people, we would not face any disappointments and hurt.

If there are no mental actions, there will be no karmic reactions. It would be a smooth sailing.

Day 21

The one who is free from desires, whose mind and senses are under control and who has renounced all proprietorship, does not incur sin by merely doing bodily action. (4.21)

Our actions are governed and defined by our thoughts. And our thoughts are a product of our mind, which is mostly influenced by our senses. The senses create desires, which result in attachment. The attachment is to the object of desire as well as the desire itself.

We buy a laptop, maybe to work from home initially. Eventually, we get dependent on our laptop for stuff other than our work, like the bank accounts, mails, photographs, social media interactions, music, movies, the works. This is attachment; it generates a feeling of comfort in us.

Now, if the laptop falls down accidentally, we would most likely panic. This is what attachment does; it creates a reaction. If, after the fall, our laptop doesn't work fully like before, we would want to buy a new one. Why? But, why not? After all, we are so dependent on it, isn't it? That's how attachment creates further desires.

If we let go of the shackles of dependency, we would become less reactive and lead a better, more peaceful life.

Day 22

All karmic bonds of a karma yogi who is free from attachment, whose mind is fixed in Self-knowledge and who does work as a service to the Lord, dissolve away. (4.23)

We know what we do consciously, because we have thought about it before actually doing it. All our lives, we think, we plan and then think more, and finally execute our thought.

Getting married, getting a job, going for higher studies, going for a holiday, buying a house or a car, even having babies is planned these days. Every thought that is based on a desire creates a bond.

Now if a person decides not to think or plan so much, they would do things differently. They would get married whenever they meet the right person. They would apply to places where they would love to work, and not necessarily to where they are expected to work.

In short, this person would not follow what everyone else around them are doing; they would carve their own path. Because there would be no pressures on them, they would be at peace.

We create our own pressures; the moment we stop doing it, we feel free.

Day 23

The Spirit shall be realized by the one who considers everything as a manifestation or an act of the Spirit. (4.24)

When the waves of an ocean rise and fall and then dash against each other, they are not creating anything new because the ocean and its waves are one. The waves form out of the ocean and merge back into it.

This is the truth of the universal Spirit residing within us and everyone else. The Spirit creates us and when we die, we merge into it, to be born again in another body.

One who understands this truth also understands that feeling happy or sad is irrelevant, that hurting someone or feeling hurt by someone's action is also irrelevant.

Every living organism has the same eventual destiny, though the paths may vary. Whoever is born, has to die. Knowing this, does it make any sense to waste time running after things or hurting people? Wouldn't it be better if we enjoyed every moment of our life?

Day 24

Those who perform selfless service obtain the nectar of Self-knowledge as a result of their sacrifice and attain the Supreme Being. Even this world is not a happy place for the non-sacrificer, how can the other world be? (4.31)

No pain no gain, goes the popular saying. We are taught to work hard from the time we are old enough to understand. As children, we are told to study hard and do well to get admissions in good universities. There also we are told to work hard to excel, to get into the profession of our choice. At our workplace too, we are expected to work hard to get promoted to finally reach the top of the rung. Working hard is synonymous with achievement.

Forming attachments is easy. But detachment needs working hard. Like they say, if you remove H from habit, a bit remains; if you remove A, bit remains; if you remove B it still remains. The point that's being made here is that any habit is very difficult to break. Attachments also are habits. We get used to desiring things and people.

Keeping a leash on our senses needs discipline. Every time we see a new model of mobile phone or anything else that the media is throwing at us 24x7, we needn't buy it. Controlling such urges, such temptations, requires intense working. We have to be convinced that the thing that is tempting us is not really needed by us. It's not need, but greed that is making us even look in that direction.

Once convinced, the battle is half won. After that it's just a matter of making a habit of saying no to temptations.

Day 25

Acquiring transcendental knowledge is superior to any material sacrifice such as doing charity. Purification of mind and intellect that eventually leads to the dawn of transcendental knowledge and Self-realization is the sole purpose of any spiritual action. (4.33)

So-and-so billionaire donated hundreds of millions to some charity in a developing country—we keep hearing this kind of stuff happening all over the globe. Most of these rich people did nothing for society when they themselves were growing. Once they felt they had more than enough—and everyone has a different parameter for that—they decided it was time for them to give it back to society.

When you share what you have in excess, what you can spare after fulfilling your needs, it is selfish charity. What Krishna talks about here is different.

When people are compassionate, they would help everyone right through their life. In their workplace they would help their subordinates when needed. At home they would look after their staff well. So, when their wealth grows, the people around them would also prosper along with them. This is selfless charity.

People can extend this kind of help when they are detached from their material wealth. This is real wisdom.

Day 26

Acquire this transcendental knowledge from a Self-realized master by humble reverence, by sincere inquiry and by service. The empowered ones, who have realized the truth, will teach you. (4.34)

When we are physically, physiologically sick, we go to a doctor. It stands to reason then that when we are mentally sick, troubled or stressed, we should seek advice from an expert in that field.

It happens in any field; we call a plumber for our house's plumbing issues or a carpenter for woodwork or furniture related queries. In our workplace too, responsibilities are delegated according to expertise.

It is seen lately that more and more people are reporting burnouts and depression at a young age. Obviously, they are unable to handle their stressful lives. At this point, they are advised de-stressing programmes, most of which use meditation to relax the person.

Why reach this point? If we can be a bit more alert towards ourselves and understand our own desires, we should be able to reason out with our own selves. Meditation teaches the same—looking inwards. Taking help from outside is great, but taking help from our own inner wisdom is the best.

Day 27

Even if one is the most sinful of all sinners, one shall yet cross over the ocean of sin by the raft of Self-knowledge alone. (4.36)

One is not born a sinner. It's the circumstances and one's reaction to those circumstances that decide the nature of the person.

A poor boy may steal because he is hungry. It is a crime for others, but not for him, as he has to satisfy his hunger or else he'll die. For him stealing is a lifesaving activity. If not helped on time, this young boy would grow up to become a bigger thief.

Most sinners start like this young boy. They commit a sin to help themselves get out of a sticky situation. Once they get away with it, it quickly becomes a habit. This is the time when intervention is required—it is like de-addiction. The sinner has to be forcibly disciplined to rid them of their addiction for sinning. It has to be done under strict monitoring.

The next step is rehabilitation. The sinner can be completely transformed, as has been seen in a number of prisons. Once free of his sinning habit, the person becomes as normal as you and me. It is like cancer. Once a person remains cancer free for five years, he is declared healthy.

Day 28

As the blazing fire reduces wood to ashes, similarly, the fire of Self-knowledge reduces all bonds of karma to ashes. (4.37)

When people start working on a computer for the first time, they fumble. For every little thing they turn to an expert for explanation. One day, they realize that working on a computer is not difficult at all. The software programs are quite user-friendly.

That's the day of enlightenment for them. Their confidence level goes up. They are now ready to teach others who are less knowledgeable than them. This is what knowledge or understanding does. It opens our eyes to see things that we had not seen earlier and hear things we had missed out on.

At a deeper level, when we understand the cosmic truth, we are enlightened. It's like shedding the veil of ignorance from around us. It's like the forest fire consuming the dead trees to make way for new ones to grow. When we understand the impermanent nature of things around us, including our own self, all our desires move away from us, leaving us free and at peace.

Day 29

There is no purifier in this world like the true knowledge of the Supreme Being. One discovers this knowledge within, naturally, in course of time when one's mind is cleansed of selfishness by karma yoga. (4.38)

Things happen when they have to happen. We cannot rush anyone's timeline. Look around at nature; can we rush the trees to bear fruit or flowers to bloom? They do that when the time is right for them to do so. It's the same with everything.

The point to be understood here is that all individuals have their own unique timeline. Some people take longer to learn while some pick up very quickly. We have seen that in school with our classmates, at home with siblings and at workplace with colleagues.

Following our own individual timeline, we reach various realizations about the impermanence of life, the cosmic truth and about the futility of pursuing the materialistic goals. And when we reach this point, our innate wisdom guides us on the right path.

The path and the destination is the same for everyone, but the time of arrival varies for each one of us.

Day 30

The one who has faith in God, is sincere in yogic practices, and has control over the mind and senses, gains this transcendental knowledge. Having gained this knowledge, one quickly attains supreme peace or liberation. (4.39)

It is our senses that create confusion in our mind. If our nose was not so good in appreciating fragrances, how would the huge perfume industry survive! Apart from food and housing, the huge amount of money that is being spent on clothes is a sheer waste. It's all because of our eyes telling us what is in fashion and what is not.

A mind that is not strong enough gets lured into the maze of temptations and loses itself there. This is known as getting addicted;

addiction is not just to alcohol or drugs, it's to clothes and jewels as well as to food.

Wise people think twice before buying anything luxurious. They do not indulge in impulsive buying. They weigh their options, study the intensity of the need and then decide. The result is almost always in negative.

A person who can control his mind can control the world, as they say. Actually such a person is detached from the worldly ties and hence cannot be controlled by anyone or anything. That is very powerful indeed. Such wise people sail through the world like a duck sails through muddy waters without getting its wings dirty.

Day 31

Work does not bind a person who has renounced work by renouncing the fruits of work through karma yoga, and whose confusion with regard to body and Spirit is completely destroyed by the application of Self-knowledge. (4.41)

Nothing can bind people who are detached from the material world. Such people are not bogged down by the responsibilities of their workplace or family. They are perpetually relaxed and go about fulfilling their duties calmly.

The wise have clarity of mind and know what their duties are. They fulfil them without asking any questions because they have no questions, no expectations; they cannot be disappointed or hurt. One who cannot be hurt is forever happy and at peace.

The wise are not affected by their senses. The material world doesn't tempt them. They know what they genuinely need and what is superfluous luxury. They are the masters of their mind and its thoughts.

Life becomes very comfortable if we have clarity in our thoughts. We know our path, we know our job, we know our goal and we work with sincerity. That's all that is required. We will reach where we are supposed to, in the time that it is supposed to take. As mentioned earlier, we cannot rush any timelines.

APRIL

Day 1

Cut the ignorance-born confusion with regard to body and Spirit by the sword of Self-knowledge, resort to karma yoga, and get up for the war. (4.42)

Ignorance is our worst enemy and education is the best weapon to destroy it. History has also shown us how education helped civilizations grow and prosper and how it helped build nations.

Without the basic knowledge of fire, we wouldn't have reached this far. Basic things like the knife we use to cut fruits and vegetables or the clothes we wear, wouldn't have been there if some people in the remote past had not felt the need to ease their situation of discomfort. The wisdom of the early humans taught them to sharpen the stone to use it to cut better.

There is no disputing the fact that even today inventions are constantly happening and they certainly are done keeping the benefit of humankind in mind.

Knowledge is so basic and yet so important. We should not underestimate the power of our intellect. We should be in constant touch with our intellect as that's our best guide to resolve problems. It is like a torch in darkness. It is our tool to cut through the web of material temptations and lead a detached and peaceful life.

5

Path of Renunciation

2–25 April

Day 2

The path of Self-knowledge and the path of selfless service both lead to the supreme goal. But of the two, the path of selfless service is superior to the path of Self-knowledge, because it is easier to practise. (5.02)

There are people who get sick and tired of their work and family pressures and decide to leave everything and go someplace remote. In ancient times, it was called sanyas. These days, people quit their job, divorce their spouse and leave the city; they go to another part of the country or the world and start afresh. This is escaping the reality. It cannot help them.

In the monasteries and ashrams, not everyone is at peace. The place does not guarantee peace, at best it just gives you space to meditate undisturbed.

However many books that a person may read and even understand, it will not help them if they don't practise what they have read. When the mind is full of all kinds emotions, meditation cannot happen. For that, one needs a quiet mind.

The wise are aware of the cosmic truth and are unattached to the emotions generated by their senses. They are in control of their mind and are devoted to selfless work. Such people do not need to go in isolation to quieten their mind; their mind is already at peace.

Day 3

A person should be considered a true renunciate who has neither attachment, nor aversion for anything. One is easily liberated from karmic bondage by becoming free from attachment and aversion. (5.03)

Physically giving up anything or any habit is never as effective as giving up from your heart. The thought of what you have renounced should not cross your mind. And even if it does, it should not affect you or generate any emotion in you.

When a person quits smoking or any other addiction, just staying away from it is not enough. True de-addiction is when seeing people smoking does not create any desire or aversion in that person.

People have a tendency to get stuck in the opposites. One day we love sweets and, when the doctor tells us we are diabetic, we start hating sweets. The bond of love has changed to hate but the bond still remains.

Being really free is when we don't experience attachment or aversion to anything or anyone. That is true renunciation. When the mind is guided by intellect, renouncing attachments becomes easy.

Day 4

The ignorant—not the wise—consider the path of Self-knowledge and the path of selfless service (karma yoga) as different from each other. The person who has truly mastered one gets the benefits of both. (5.04)

Everyone in the world has the same goal in life—to be happy. Some raise a family to feel happy, some follow their passion of dancing or theatre to be happy, some are sportspersons, some businesspersons and some professionals. People try to follow the path that gives them happiness. Earning money is very important but the underlying purpose of living life day to day is to find happiness.

In pursuit of happiness, some get lost. They get trapped in a maze of temptations. One day they realize their folly and want to leave it all and disappear. This is not possible for obvious reasons; everyone has certain obligations to their family. Obviously, these people do not know that by using their intellect, they could get out of their trap successfully.

Our intellect teaches us the wisdom of mentally isolating ourselves from the material world's temptations. Physical isolation is not required. Having accomplished mental isolation, it is easier to continue working as usual, except this time it would be selfless and not motivated by some material desire. The result would be the otherwise elusive happiness.

Day 5

Whatever goal a renunciate reaches, a karma yogi also reaches the same goal. Therefore, the one who sees the path of renunciation and the path of unselfish work as the same, really sees. (5.05)

Two friends studying together in school decide to become doctors to help poor people. They study hard and become doctors. One step covered, the next step was to help the poor who could not afford hospital treatment.

One of the friends was wealthy, so he built a hospital and created a special wing to give free treatment to poor patients. He ran the rest of the hospital commercially and used part of the profits to treat the poor patients.

The other friend did not have the means to set up even a clinic. He left home and went to a village to serve people. There he lived and looked after the villagers, free of cost. People would get cured and pay him with grains, fruits, etc.

Both the friends achieved their purpose, but by following different paths. The important thing is to understand the purpose. The purpose should not be sense gratification, it should be selfless service, and only then will it result in immense satisfaction and happiness.

Day 6

True renunciation of action is difficult to attain without performance of action. A sage devoted to action quickly attains nirvana. (5.06)

A person who doesn't sing at all can't give up singing. They have to be doing it to be giving it up. One has to be wealthy to renounce wealth, like Buddha did.

All the trappings of wealth, in terms of beautiful clothes, servants at beck and call, all the possible gadgets, the best of cars and more money than would ever be needed, surround a wealthy person. They are the real traps. These attachments become such a part of one's life that one starts to believe that they are necessities. To renounce this kind of life takes immense mental strength. The fact that a person is able to do it means they are in control of their mind. This is the first step towards attaining everlasting happiness.

The next step is for humans to understand that what they have to do should be done with utmost sincerity. If they are teachers, they have to teach with full dedication and commitment. They should not worry about promotions and competition from their colleagues. Their selfless commitment to teaching would filter down to their students whose performance would pick up. It's amazing how these things are so contagious! Such detached renunciates would forever be at peace with themselves and the world around them.

Day 7

A karma yogi, whose mind is pure, whose mind and senses are under control, and who sees one and the same Spirit in all beings, is not bound by karma, though engaged in work. (5.07)

We constantly hear stories about how a milk vendor's son or a carpenter's daughter have become a doctor or a civil engineer. These stories keep reiterating the fact that every human is the same, regardless of their background.

Human aspirations remain the same; the means may or may not be available to fulfil them. Some would steal or cheat to get the means; others would work hard and patiently muster up enough means to get them on the path of their aspirations.

When we are in control of our senses, we become more alert about our surroundings. It's like the driver who is in complete control of the vehicle he is driving. He is able to look around and appreciate the scenery on the way, as well as avoid the potholes on the road and stop at the traffic lights.

Likewise, in life in general, and in the workplace in particular, mindfulness helps us to understand our subordinates better. We would then be able to help them better. Our reason would not be that helping them is going to help us in some way, but we would help them because they need help.

Day 8

The wise person who knows the truth thinks, 'I do nothing at all'. In seeing, hearing, touching, smelling, eating, walking, sleeping, breathing, speaking, etc., the wise person believes that only the senses are operating upon their objects. (5.08–5.09)

It is humility that makes a man an angel, they say. It is true, humility is wisdom. It is the knowledge that the same universal energy flows in everyone and that we are doing what we are supposed to do. We are but a pawn in the larger scheme of things.

If we track down the biographies of successful people, we would notice that most of them were totally focussed on their path and did whatever they did without thinking how it would benefit them individually. They worked for the benefit of humankind.

Absolute selfless devotion to their work and detachment from the material world was the secret of their success. Considering they were detached from everything, they were also detached from their success. This endearing quality is humility.

Some successful people fail at this point. They start believing that they have some superhuman quality or talent to make them reach where they have. They forget that there were a whole lot people who supported them. After all, behind every successful person are his or her family, colleagues or subordinates and many more.

The wise are always grateful for all the support they get from everywhere and everyone.

Day 9

One who does all work as an offering to God—abandoning selfish attachment to results—remains untouched by karmic reaction or sin as a lotus never gets wet by water. (5.10)

The lotus remains unsoiled while floating on muddy water. This is how a wise man lives in the material world, unaffected by sensory temptations. Some people are very excitable. The smallest of things, like watching a film, stirs them emotionally. The turmoil of the world around them affects them easily. Such people are obviously like puppets in the hands of their senses.

On the other hand, people who have a grip on their senses and their emotions are calm and collected in any situation. They move on through life working selflessly. These people remain unaffected through the ups and downs of life.

Since these people are not doing anything for a selfish purpose, they can do nothing wrong. And since they are selfless, they do not have any expectations from anyone or anything, which translates to absence of disappointment or anger or any other emotion. These wise people are successful humans and great leaders.

Day 10

The karma yogis perform action only for the purification of their mind and intellect, without selfish attachment with their body, mind, intellect and senses. (5.11)

We do not realize how and when we get caught up in the material web. It starts innocently. It could be a gift, like a shirt, which we enjoy wearing because it looks good and is of good quality. Once it gets old, we want to replace it with something similar, something as good.

It is evident that we have become attached to the shirt, though unconsciously. We desire to experience yet again, the feeling that the shirt gave us. This can happen with anything. Desires are generated by our senses in response to material triggers. Attachments result from these desires and we get caught in between the two.

The wise know the dangers of getting attached, so they do not get attached to the comfort provided by the shirt. They understand that material comforts do not last for long. This shirt will get old and will be discarded; a new one will take its place, then that one will become old and another one will come…this will go on. The wise carry on with their lives, unattached to anything.

Day 11

A karma yogi attains unshakable peace by abandoning attachment to the fruits of work while others, who are attached to the fruits of work, become bound by selfish work. (5.12)

Peace is freedom from disturbance. It's the state of mind of a person who does not get agitated by any disturbing thoughts. With the kind of lives we live, such a state of mind is not at all easy to attain.

The moment a baby is born, parents start fretting for its admission in school; the fretting continues till the child is in college. After that, a new kind of stress enters the picture, that of making a career.

These stresses become a part of a person's life, so much so, that they wouldn't know how to pass their time if there's nothing to stress about. It may seem funny but it's a serious malady. We are bound by and bound to the world that we have created for ourselves. In the tight schedule of our life, we have not left any window for peace.

The only way to achieve unshakable peace would be to detach ourselves from everything. If there's no attachment to manipulate us, we will be able to walk steadily, peacefully and happily.

Day 12

The Lord neither creates the urge for action, nor the feeling of doership, nor the attachment to the results of action in people. The delusive material world does all these. (5.14)

We may not realize it, but actually at all times, the choice of doing anything is with us. Whether it's the big decisions of our life or the small ones, the choice is ours. Even the choice of allowing someone else to decide for us is our choice.

In a simple situation, when we feel hot, we switch on the fan or when we feel hungry, we eat food. Let us look at it differently. We feel hot and react to the discomfort that heat is causing to us. In order to relieve ourselves from the discomfort, we switch on the fan. We can tolerate the discomfort, ignore it and not switch on the fan. It's up to us, isn't it?

It is easier to understand with hunger and food. When we are fasting, don't we ignore our hunger pangs? We are in control then. If we could have such control over all our senses, we would be in control of our actions.

We are surrounded by temptations in this material world. It is our choice to succumb or not to succumb. If we succumb, we fall into the trap of like-dislike, creating disturbing thoughts in our mind. The way to get rid of this disturbance is in our hands—by detaching ourselves from the material world.

Day 13

The Lord does not take the responsibility for the good or evil deeds of anybody. The veil of ignorance covers Self-knowledge; thereby people become deluded and do evil deeds. (5.15)

People generally like to blame others for whatever that goes wrong in their own lives. Everyone is looking for a scapegoat to pin the blame on. It could be a family member, teacher, friend, colleague, management of the company or even the government.

When they are unable to find anyone to blame, they turn to God and ask, 'Why me?' They are so blinded by the worldly illusions that they are unable to see the genesis of their troubles. They firmly believe that whatever they have done thus far is justified. And, if certain things are not working out according to them or going against them, then surely it cannot be their fault. It has to be someone else's.

Such a delusional state continues forever, unless the individual honestly starts looking inwards. Once that happens, the person wakes up to reality. This is enlightenment.

The wise, the enlightened, understand that the material world will always throw temptations at them; it's up to them to remain unaffected and continue walking their path. Even the most evil people can wise up to this truth and change their lives completely.

Day 14

Transcendental knowledge destroys the ignorance of the Spirit and reveals the Supreme Being just as the sun reveals the beauty of the objects of the world. (5.16)

An egocentric person is actually ignorant and not as highly intelligent as they believe themself to be. Actually, most people misunderstand the meaning of intelligence—they relate it to education. They forget that intelligence is the inherent nature of human beings; education adds information. It's the intellect that teaches us how to use our native intelligence.

Dhirubhai Ambani, the father of Reliance Industries, was a college dropout and Walt Disney was a high school dropout. These are classic examples showing that education and success need not be related.

People also connect intelligence with success; that is also not true. Success is transitory—a truly intelligent person knows that. Success has the tendency to go to the head, it is said, which is true. Once they experience success, people tend to believe that success is for keeps and that they have become infallible. Such egocentric people are the most ignorant of all.

Everything has a fixed life. Whatever is born has to die; be it success or failure, they end eventually. The wise know this truth and are unattached to their success. Knowledge of this truth is the real knowledge, which removes ignorance and frees us from the shackles of illusion.

Day 15

Those people whose mind and intellect are totally merged in the Supreme Being, those who are firmly devoted to and have God as their main goal and sole refuge, and whose impurities are destroyed by the knowledge of the Self, do not take birth again. (5.17)

Some people, though rare, complete their studies and join a workplace to earn a living. They continue working in the same place till their retirement. Their colleagues provoke them to participate in office politics, but they remain unconcerned.

At home, their parents, spouse and children goad them to find a better job, but they remain unaffected. Such people are a satisfied lot. Their goal in life is to provide for their family, which they do satisfactorily. They don't understand any other kind of goal.

Material goods do not tempt these people; their happiness comes from a job well done. In good times and in adverse, these people remain calm and handle the situation with equanimity.

Since they are detached from sensory desires, they are at peace. They do not run after sensory pleasures like others, but sit back and smile in the knowledge of the futility of the unending chase. These people do not generate any karmic reactions and hence become free from the cycle of rebirths.

Day 16

An enlightened person—by perceiving God in all—looks at a learned person, an outcast or even a cow, an elephant or a dog, with an equal eye. (5.18)

An eddy is a current, of water or air, moving in a direction that is different from the main current. Eddies can commonly be seen in rivers and oceans. When we look at an eddy from up close, it seems like an independent body of water, with its own path and purpose. But when we step back and see the entire picture, we see the eddy as just a little patch in the large river, starting from and merging into it seamlessly.

Quantum physicist David Bohm postulated, 'The entire universe must, on a very accurate level, be regarded as a single indivisible unit.'[1] Earlier Einstein had also said that energy and matter are the same things, just in different forms. Science has proved that the same energy source permeates everything, only the forms and shapes vary.

The wise are aware of this truth and treat everyone the same. It is the ignorant who treat people on the basis of their colour, gender, caste and class. The perception of differences is the cause of ego, of self-importance. And the ego is the cause of all despair.

---

[1] David Bohm, *Quantum Theory*; Prentice-Hall: Englewood Cliffs, USA, 1951.

Day 17

Everything has been accomplished in this very life by the one whose mind is set in equality. Such a person has realized the Supreme Being, because the Supreme Being is flawless and impartial. (5.19)

We live our entire lives counting our accomplishments in the form of our successes or the successes of our children. We tend to believe that our children are our products and hence their success or failure reflects on us. And of course, the parameters of success always remain how much one has achieved in life in terms of fame and wealth.

We believe that fame and wealth make a person happy. Do they really? Because, if it is so, then why do the wealthy start philanthropic activities once their needs are assuaged? Most of them do that.

They realize at some point that somehow their wealth is not making them happy or even satisfied. They also realize that wealth has a limited use as far as their personal needs go. After their personal needs are taken care of, their time is spent in protecting their wealth, which then becomes a cause of stress.

The wise do not reach this point in their lives. They know nothing is theirs to amass and all gets left behind when they die. Like a riverbed that remains still under the ever-changing flow of water, the wise remain undisturbed by the ever-changing life around them.

Day 18

One who neither rejoices on obtaining what is pleasant, nor grieves on obtaining the unpleasant, who has a steady mind, who is not deluded, and who is a knower of the Supreme Being, such a person eternally abides with the Supreme Being. (5.20)

Detachment is the key to eternal peace and joy. But then, people misunderstand the meaning of detachment. They think a detached person is cold-blooded and emotionless. It is far from the truth.

A detached person goes through all the emotions but does not get attached to any of them. Feeling an emotion is different from retaining the feeling in memory. When we retain the memory of a feeling, good or bad, we are actually getting attached to that emotion. The emotion then controls us; we remember the emotion and the associated feeling surfaces. This is how the emotion, as memory, controls us.

When a subordinate misbehaves and is pulled up for their action, the story should end there. But if the boss continues to remember the incident and hold a grudge against the subordinate, he's making his own life hell.

The wise are detached. They neither feel elated, nor do they feel depressed by the ups and downs of life. They live in the moment and move on when the moment passes. They are aware that all good or bad times end, as do the days and nights. This awareness brings immense peace and joy.

Day 19

Such a person, who is unattached to external sensual pleasures, is in union with the Supreme Being and discovers the joy of the Self through contemplation, enjoying transcendental bliss. (5.21)

We are aware that if our mind is not occupied by multiple tasks, we always perform the task at hand better. Our concentration or focus is better when we plan or work on one job at a time or study one subject at a time.

Whether at home or at workplace, we keep fumbling, forgetting important things when we are distracted with too many issues. Sounds familiar?

The opposite is true as well. When we are at ease, with no issues to worry about, children sorted, bills paid, no backlog pending from work, we start getting interesting ideas or brainwaves, as some might like to call them. We get brainwaves about how to renovate our house, where to go for the weekend break, a new story idea to pitch to a studio...it could be anything. We are at our creative best when our minds are uncluttered.

At a macro level, if we permanently declutter our mind, getting rid of all attachments, we would find our lives simplified and eternally blissful.

Day 20

Sensual pleasures are verily the source of misery, and have a beginning and an end. Therefore, the wise do not rejoice in sensual pleasures. (5.22)

If we look around, we see the material world, our world of conveniences. This world has made us dependant on it without us realizing it. And it's not that these things of convenience, which make our life simpler, last forever. They don't. The gadgets keep breaking down or the technology becomes obsolete. The commonest examples staring at us are our laptops and mobile phones.

The sources of convenience or pleasure also have their side-effects. First we buy packaged food like frozen vegetables or canned beans for convenience of cooking. Then a study surfaces that packaged foods are harmful for health in the long run.

This is true for every sensory pleasure. The movies end, the food is finished, the perfumes get over, the clothes fade, the flowers die... the list is never ending. Finally, after accumulating, looking after and replenishing all the objects of sensual pleasures in our life, life leaves us. The wise know this truth and, therefore, remain unaffected by the sensual pleasures.

Day 21

One who finds happiness within, who rejoices within, and who is illuminated by Self-knowledge—such a yogi attains nirvana and goes to the Supreme Being. (5.24)

As long as we have any material desires, we have to work towards fulfilling them. We are absorbed in our attachment to those desires, the fulfilment of which becomes our goal in life. Things don't come easy; we may fail many times before succeeding.

How many of us take failures kindly? There is so much competition out there and in that crowd only a handful rise to the top. Life becomes a race. Even thinking about it makes one stressed. The definition of happiness changes from moment to moment, keeping in pace with the ever-changing material world around us.

The wise understand the true nature of happiness. The ordinary sensual objects of the world do not give any joy to them, as they know the ephemeral nature of these objects. In their understanding of the cosmic truth lies everlasting happiness.

Day 22

Seers, whose sins (or imperfections) are destroyed, whose doubts have been dispelled by Self-knowledge, whose minds are disciplined, and who are engaged in the welfare of all beings, attain the Supreme Being. (5.25)

Most people, when they start working, work with the intent of earning their living. They need money to look after their primary needs of food, shelter and clothing. The solution of finding a job to pay for our basic needs is also the starting point of all our problems in life. How?

With the leftover money in hand, we start looking around. Temptations are everywhere; the world is one big shopping mall. We start listening to people, start copying what others are doing, and slowly, we lose our own identity. We stop using our own brain and become sheep to anyone who wants to lead us into further temptations.

But then, there are some who wake up one day to realize where they are going wrong. And they stop. This realization is the first step towards attaining wisdom. The wise understand that the sensual pleasures are like mirages; they exist only in the eyes and not in reality. They turn away from these mirages and look towards those who need their help.

Day 23

Those who are free from lust and anger, who have subdued the mind and senses, and who have known the Self, easily attain nirvana. (5.26)

All living beings need air to breathe and food to stay alive. A need is a necessity. Once it is fulfilled, it gets over, technically. But the senses are so clever that they keep pulling us towards temptations, convincing us that they are needed.

For instance, when we see the advertisements of all kinds of foods, which ones fall under the head of necessary foods? Only the staples. What about the rest? The rest are meant to tempt our taste buds—they are luxuries. Eventually, seeing these foods, we start believing that they are somehow necessary.

Similarly, larger expenses like those on houses are initially need-based, but eventually become vanity-based. We do not get to know when our need becomes lust. Tragically, once lust comes into the picture, it always brings with it anger. The passion that converts need to lust is also the driving force behind the anger that results when the lust is not fulfilled.

A person, who is in control of his senses, is free from lust and anger. Such a wise person is always at peace with himself and the world around him.

Day 24

A sage is liberated by renouncing all sense enjoyments, fixing the eyes and the mind on an imaginary black dot between the eyebrows, equalizing the breath moving through the nostrils by using yogic techniques, keeping the senses, mind and intellect under control, having salvation as the prime goal, and by becoming free from lust, anger and fear. (5.27–5.28)

Detachment is not easy to come by. But once we understand its importance, we can surely try to consciously develop the habit of detaching ourselves from the world around us.

The external world of material objects cannot harm us unless we engage with it physically or mentally. Even if we abstain physically, the mental engagement itself causes disturbance in our life. The only way to get away from it all is to disengage ourselves mentally.

Just like we need to exercise our body to tone it and keep it healthy and fit, so do we need to exercise our mind to maintain its strength. Meditation may not be easy for most; it is advised to prepare the body physically first.

Simple things like fixing our gaze in-between our eyebrows helps to steady the eyeballs. This, followed by conscious breathing, helps in steadying our breath. This exercise quietens the mind.

Once our mind is calm and quiet, we are able see things better and understand the difference between need and lust. This clarity is essential to detach ourselves from the sensory temptations surrounding us.

Day 25

A true yogi observes me in all beings and also sees every being in me. Indeed, the Self-realized person sees me, the same Supreme Lord, everywhere. (5.29)

True liberation is when we begin to see others as ourselves. This is when the concept of ego disappears from our mind and we remain unaffected by desire and anger.

When we consciously renounce the sensory temptations, we regain control of our own mind. Once the mind is calm, the truth appears. The truth is that the same energy source flows through everyone and that all material things are ephemeral.

In a workplace, as a boss or leader, we should pause and observe everything around us. We would realize that every team member is inherently the same, with the same reactions and emotions, though their skillsets might be totally different from each other. We would also realize that people are dispensable; they might come and go but the organization remains. And one day, the organization also ceases to exist.

We would realize that instead of getting caught up in petty issues, we must continue working selflessly towards the larger goal, one that benefits the entire humankind.

6

Path of Meditation

26 April–25 May

Day 26

One who performs the prescribed duty without seeking its fruit for personal enjoyment is a renunciate and a karma yogi. One does not become a renunciate merely by not lighting the fire, and one does not become a yogi merely by abstaining from work. (6.01)

When people hear about detachment, they feel the easiest way to detach is to get away. They feel if they stay away from the object of desire, the attachment would wane and disappear. But out of sight, out of mind doesn't work for desires.

Desires stem from our senses and feed off our mind. They have the power to control us through our mind. And, no matter how far we run away physically, we carry our minds with us. A person who is trying to quit smoking or is fasting would always be thinking about smoking or food.

Detachment is lack of any attachment to the object of desire even when it is in front of you. The person who has really quit smoking for good does not get tempted even when he sees his friends smoking.

Detachment is very powerful, as a detached person is in complete control of themselves, even while surrounded by temptations of this material world. That is their way of enjoying life.

Day 27

Renunciation is the same as karma yoga because no one becomes a karma yogi who has not renounced the selfish motive behind an action. (6.02)

Detachment should not be confused with renunciation of the material world. A detached person is not an ochre-clad hermit. A detached person is the coolest person you'll come across, one who is grounded even when they are the peak of their career.

People like Mahatma Gandhi or Mother Teresa worked selflessly for others. They devoted their lives working tirelessly for a cause. They were karma yogis. They had renounced all selfish motives and had no material desires. They were in full control of their minds.

Being selflessly devoted to work is as good as renouncing the world because selfless devotion requires a certain discipline, which in turn requires controlling of sensual desires.

A successful CEO of a company is the most disciplined of all its workers. After all, he has to run the company and take it to the top of the ladder, amidst all the competition in the market. He cannot achieve that if petty attachments distract him. Though we call such people cold-blooded and ruthless, they are actually detached.

Day 28

For the wise, who seek to attain yoga of meditation or the equanimity of mind, karma yoga is said to be the means. For the one who has attained yoga, equanimity becomes the means of Self-realization. A person is said to have attained yogic perfection when he or she has no desire for sensual pleasures or attachment to the fruits of work and has renounced all personal selfish motives. (6.03–6.04)

The most popular treatment or solution for any kind of issue these days is meditation, so much so, that a number of workplaces have started having meditation rooms too. This is because stress has been discovered to be at the root of every mental and physical ailment. And stress is the result of unfulfilled expectations.

At home, the demands or requirements of our family are never-ending. At work, it's the same; there are company targets and personal goals to be achieved and we're under constant scrutiny of our bosses as well as colleagues. There always seems to be a fire-fighting-like situation. All that, plus the commute and mismanaged meal timings; it's a perfect recipe for a body and mind breakdown.

The wise do not have any expectations and are unaffected by the expectations of others. This attitude helps them to maintain their balance of mind and lead a happy and healthy life, even amidst the chaos.

Day 29

One must be elevated, and not degraded, by one's own mind. The mind alone is one's friend as well as one's enemy. The mind is the friend of those who have control over it and the mind acts like an enemy for those who do not control it. (6.05–6.06)

Our minds are the most powerful part of our body system. Human body works like a team, with each organ carrying out its designated function without any pause. The heart pumps blood round the clock, the lungs breathe and our other systems like the digestive, excretory and endocrine, also function 24×7.

It's only our mind that is mostly restless. It keeps thinking endlessly about everything. Some of these thoughts are helpful, but some are not. The helpful or positive thoughts push us to do great things in life and achieve fame. The negative thoughts make us jealous or angry with others and this may lead to arguments or fights.

The negative thoughts pull us down, while the positive ones pull us up. This is how we swing when our mind is controlling us. It's not wrong to say 'It's all in the mind'—because it is. Our mind can make or break us.

Normally, the mind is controlled by our senses. The senses tempt the mind into getting attached to the objects of desire. We need to be in control of our mind and firmly prevent it from falling prey to the sensual desires. This is what the wise do. For the wise, the mind becomes their friend; as for the fools, it becomes an enemy.

Day 30

One who has control over the mind is tranquil in heat and cold, in pleasure and pain, and in honour and dishonour, and remains ever steadfast with the supreme Self. (6.07)

Meditation helps to slow down thoughts. With less traffic of thoughts, the mind also relaxes. A relaxed mind is open to wisdom. Only when the water is calm can it reflect the moon.

However much we train our mind to remain calm and unaffected through the external disturbances of the world around us, the inner disturbance is the toughest to handle.

Our body can be trained to be indifferent to heat and cold, pleasure and pain. But what about the words spoken by others that remain lodged in our minds? We need to train our mind to let go of the reactions that are created by other people's words. The mind would certainly react, but then, it needs to move on.

We have to train our minds to be smooth like glass, so that thoughts, reactions and emotions come and slip away; nothing stays back. The wise remain calm in every situation, because nothing remains in their minds for long.

MAY

Day 1

A person who has both Self-knowledge and Self-realization, who is equanimous, who has control over the mind and senses, and to whom a clod of earth, a stone and gold are the same is called a yogi. (6.08)

An ironsmith puts hot pieces of iron on an anvil to hammer them into the desired shapes. The anvil itself is made of iron, but does not get affected by the intense hammering. Likewise, a detached person's mind remains unaffected by the intense onslaught of material temptations surrounding him.

The wise are aware of the true nature of everything. They know that the same energy forms a clod of earth or a stone or a piece of gold. This has now been proved by science as well. Having this knowledge, the wise give equal importance to the three.

Once we are able to see everything and everyone in the same light, we stop discriminating, which is a huge step towards peaceful cohabitation in the world.

The next step is the understanding that everything and everyone in this world has a fixed, limited lifespan. Nothing remains forever, including us. This understanding enables us to not indulge in any attachments.

Day 2

A person is considered superior who is impartial towards companions, friends, enemies, neutrals, arbiters, haters, relatives, saints and sinners. (6.09)

One of the very important characteristics of a successful leader is impartiality. An effective leader does not indulge in favouritism. His equal treatment of his subordinates gets him their sworn loyalty.

In life too, we come across people who could be honest or corrupt. We may have been mistreated by many during our course of work or otherwise. As we go along in life, we unconsciously start slotting people under the ones we like and those we don't. There could even be a third category of people we hate.

These emotional labels are actually a form of attachment to those people. The fact that we hate a person indicates towards that person's influence on us. It shows that we have empowered that person to create the emotion of hate in us. Like this, we create innumerable bonds in our mind that ultimately create disturbances. This is how we get caught in a rut and do not come to know till our stress manifests as disease.

The best course of action would be to stop judging people. If we stop getting affected by people and their actions, we stop judging them. And if we do not judge them, it's easy for us to ignore them and move on. It's simple. If we ignore our enemies, they cease to exist.

Day 3

A yogi, seated in solitude, should constantly try to contemplate on the majesty of the Supreme Being after bringing the mind and senses under control, and becoming free from desires and proprietorship. (6.10)

A man designs a couple of beautiful bags and decides to set up a workshop to get them made. Once done, he shows the bags to his friends who love them. The bags get sold fast and the person feels that this success could and should be replicated.

It is obvious that this person is now entering a quagmire. He expands his operations, puts a label on his products and starts selling worldwide. He becomes the label himself; that's what happens with all the top designers. After amassing a great deal of wealth, and looking at his name staring from all the big stores all across the globe, the person starts believing that he has immortalized himself.

Unfortunately, by now, in his long and eventful journey, he has forgotten who all helped him to become what he is today. It takes one mishap by one person to bring down the whole company. Our man also gets caught up in a court case and realizes the hard facts, though a bit too late.

'Pride comes before a fall'—this actually happens. The wise

remain unattached to their success and do not consider themselves to be the doers.

Day 4

This is not possible for the one who eats too much or who does not eat at all, who sleeps too much or too little. (6.16)

Balance of mind is not restricted to the mind alone. It also includes overall balance or discipline in all our activities. This is natural, because all the voluntary activities are controlled by the mind.

The involuntary activities of our body like breathing, digesting food, etc., are, as the term implies, automatic or reflexive. We are not conscious of these activities. But all the other activities involve thinking and reasoning. We are consciously involved with the activities. So, this is where our intellect comes into play. We reason out the pros and cons before we take any action.

At this stage of reasoning, we need to understand balance, the middle path between two extremes of like-dislike, pleasure-pain, and so on. For example, instead of choosing the path of 'pleasure of eating', or the path of 'pain of starving', it would be sensible to choose neither and walk on the middle path of eating as per the need of our body.

Detachment makes us choose the middle path. Once we control our senses and get rid of attachments, we find ourselves walking the middle path, detached, and at peace.

Day 5

The yoga of meditation destroys all sorrow for the one who is moderate in eating, recreation, working, sleeping and waking. (6.17)

The world throws at us so many temptations that it is difficult to ignore them. But then, why ignore them at all? Go buy a beautiful dress, but buy only one. The idea is not to throttle or suppress your desires but to experience them and then let go of them. Attachment to the objects of desire is the root cause of all misery.

When we get attached, we want to preserve that emotion; we want more and more of it. If you open your closet and see, you will find more clothes and shoes than you actually need. You would see stuff that you haven't used for years. Why do you have all that? How did it come? It came from your greed of wanting more.

This is true for everything; be it eating or exercising; anything in excess is as harmful as lack of the same thing. The trick is moderation. If we do sufficient exercise and eat what is sufficient for our body's needs, we would not fall sick. People often fall sick because of either overeating or starving themselves.

If we maintain a work-life balance, we get to lead a mentally and physically happier and healthier life. The key is to know when to stop.

Day 6

A person is said to have achieved yoga, the union with the Spirit, when the perfectly disciplined mind becomes free from all desires and gets completely united with the Spirit in trance. (6.18)

We have seen, time and again, that it is the uncontrolled mind that wanders in search of satisfaction from the sensory pleasures. The pleasures themselves are not bad; it is their indulgence in excess that is bad.

When we crack a successful deal, we feel a sense of achievement. We celebrate that; but the celebrations cannot go on forever. Likewise, our sense of achievement too should be kept aside and we should move on to the next deal. But what happens is that people tend to remember their achievements, becoming attached to it.

We lock up many such incidents in our memory and recall them to feel good about ourselves. What is this, if not an attachment to memories and a desire to feel good?

Obvious sensory pleasures like eating, drinking, shopping, having sex, are there for all to see. But what about seeking validation, angling for compliments, expecting rewards and awards? People go to great lengths for these hidden but deep-seated desires. To be at peace within, one has to get rid of all desires, obvious and hidden.

Day 7

A lamp in a spot sheltered by the Spirit from the wind of desires does not flicker. This metaphor is used for the subdued mind of a yogi practising meditation on the Spirit. (6.19)

The flame of a lamp flickers in the wind. In the same way, the human mind also flickers in the face of many temptations. To see anything in the dark, we need a steady light. A flickering flame does not give steady light. In fact, the flickering light creates more confusion. In order to utilize the light of the flame, we need to shelter it from the wind. Once it stabilizes, it gives out steady light, helping us to see things around it.

Our mind is also like that. A flickering, restless mind is of no use. Such a mind cannot focus on one thing or make a firm decision. In order to use our mind effectively, we need to stop its wavering. Self-discipline makes the mind strong.

Thinking with a cool head is always recommended. This is because a calm mind can focus on issues and resolve them quickly. Decisions made by a wavering mind almost always turn out to be wrong whereas those taken by a calm mind always lead to success. This is applicable in all situations, at home or at work.

Day 8

When the mind, disciplined by the practice of meditation becomes steady, the ego perceives itself as soul, and one becomes content beholding the Spirit of God within. (6.20)

There are two kinds of people, extroverts and introverts. They handle their lives and its related issues differently. So, in order to calm down the mind, the extroverts would seek external help. They would do intense physical exercise, jog, play sports or indulge in any other physically tiring work.

The introverts, on the other hand, would prefer to go for long walks alone, sit by the side of a pond, write, paint or listen to soft music—basically spend time doing something alone. They are also inclined towards meditation as a means to quieten the mind.

Once the mind is quietened enough, the realization dawns that we have all come from the same source of energy and will merge with the same when we die. This humbling thought destroys the ego. Once that happens, we lose interest in the sensory desires and all attachments fall away. We get into a permanent state of contentment.

At home, when we realize and accept the fact that fretting about our child's admission will not result in him getting admitted into the college of their choice, we relax. At work too, getting stressed about our promotion is unlikely to affect our boss. Once we accept these facts, our stresses and mental confusions will disappear.

Day 9

One feels infinite bliss that is perceivable only through the intellect, and is beyond the reach of the senses. After realizing the absolute reality, one is never separated from it. (6.21)

Right from our childhood, we have been facing confusions. It could be while studying for exams, as to which subject to start first or which chapter. Later on, it becomes bigger, when we are asked to choose a career path. Very few are firm in the knowledge about what they want to do as a profession. Finally, when the person settles in the work that they love doing, they are the happiest. So, if a doctor stops working at a hospital and starts working in films, their family might be shocked but the doctor would be at peace.

Realization of truth always results in peace. It's commonly believed that truth is always bitter but it's not. The same truth can be bitter for one and sweet for the other, it's a matter of perspective. All truths, when they come to light, make our mental confusions disappear.

If the family gets to know the truth about their father's financial woes, they might feel disappointed at first. But then, they would have a clarity that they should not put any pressure on their father any more. Understanding and acceptance of reality leads to mental peace.

Day 10

Once the yogi finds the state that he considers as the treasure beyond treasures, he remains anchored in that and is immune to even the mightiest grief. (6.22)

When we are satisfied with our knowledge, we become confident to face the world. We can then face the toughest of exams without feeling a twinge of nervousness. This happens in every area of our life. It could be cooking, stitching, gardening, driving, drawing, painting—any area at all. The key is conviction. If we are convinced of our own expertise, then nobody can shake our confidence.

At a macro level, once we understand that everything in the world is perishable and dispensable, we start seeing things in a different light. And once our mind is in control of our senses instead of the other way round, we know that our happiness is in our own hands.

Armed with this knowledge, no calamity in the world can affect us. After all, it's up to us to allow anything to affect us, isn't it?

Day 11

The state of severance of union with sorrow is called yoga. This yoga should be practised with firm determination and without any mental reservation. (6.23)

It is important to continue working with dedication and full commitment, and not have any sort of doubts or reservations about the path or the outcome. When an artist is making a painting or a sculptor is chiselling stone, they do not know how beautiful their creation is going to be. They just carry on with their work, pouring their heart and soul into it.

Any kind of work should be done with such dedication. Imagine a workplace where every person is totally dedicated to their work and nobody is distracted by what the other is doing. There would be no petty politics and the end result would be success and an all-round growth of the company. But such utopian conditions are rare to come by.

Collectively it might be difficult, but individually we can practise to detach ourselves from the fruits of all our actions. Having achieved that, we would be free from all sorrow.

Day 12

One gradually attains tranquillity of mind by totally abandoning all selfish desires, completely restraining the senses from sense objects and keeping the mind fully absorbed in the Spirit by means of a well-trained intellect. (6.24-25)

As children we have done experiments in school. One of them was to study decantation. A little bit of soil is mixed with clean water in a glass, stirred and set aside. It is seen that gradually the soil particles start settling down in the bottom of the glass. Eventually, the soil settles down completely, leaving clear water that can be decanted into another glass.

Our minds are similar. They are full of stored memories and thoughts that whirl around all the time. Just as the muddy water is not of much use, so is the case with a muddled mind.

In order to use water, we need to be sure that it's clean. Since water is essential to all forms of life, we need to clean it carefully. Everyone is aware of the ill-effects of impure water.

Likewise, in order for the mind to be effectively useful and life-sustaining, we need to clean it thoroughly. The first step towards that would be to still the mind, so that all the swirling thoughts settle down. When the mind is quiet, it can focus all its energies on the task at hand.

Day 13

Wheresoever this restless and unsteady mind wanders away, one should gently bring it back to the reflection of God. (6.26)

Since the mind is a flow of thoughts, it is likely to be restless and unsteady. It is not unusual to be distracted by thoughts other than work while in the workplace. If we have to pick our child from a dance class or attend to a sick spouse or parent, the related thoughts are bound to be on the top of our mind while working.

These are our attachments. We bind ourselves to these tasks, and when their thoughts keep surfacing through the day, we get stressed. Our priorities get mixed up.

If doing a particular task is on top of our priorities, then we must find ways to delegate the other tasks to others. We can hire extra help to pick and drop our child or to look after the sick spouse or parent. Unfortunately, we don't do this as we are trapped in the emotions of relationships, yet we complain and get stressed as our work suffers because of these disturbances in our routine.

The day we decide to detach ourselves from relationships, we would not be governed by emotions and would be able to handle these issues practically. It's always the emotions that drag us down, not the task at hand.

Day 14

Supreme bliss comes to a Self-realized yogi whose mind is tranquil, whose desires are under control and who is free from faults. (6.27)

When the mental agitation or thought flow ends, the mind becomes still. This requires repeated mental efforts. We can get rid of specific attachments, for instance those to material possessions, fairly easily. It is just a question of understanding the ephemeral nature of the material objects.

Thoughts are like a bunch of horses pulling the chariot we are riding on in multiple directions. It's up to us to become a good charioteer or driver and control and drive those horses in unison. Only then can we reach our destination.

Controlling one sense is simpler like a driver controlling the car he's driving. But we are talking about the five senses. Naturally, they would pull us in five directions of temptations.

The sensory desires are very distracting. Right in the middle of our work, hunger pangs or a stink from the restroom close by or a beautiful colleague or music from a neighbour's computer or lack of proper air-conditioning can distract us, slow us down or even derail us completely. A truly tranquil mind is unaffected by any distractions.

Day 15

Such a sinless yogi, who constantly engages his or her mind and intellect with the Spirit, easily enjoys the infinite bliss of contact with the Spirit. (6.28)

Some people like to stay away from the objects of desire and distraction in order to concentrate on their work. It is a good beginning. It helps to have a workplace dedicated to our work, where we follow a timetable to discipline our senses. Having fixed mealtimes is a great way to demolish the untimely urges to eat.

This is the reason why artists and other creative people prefer to work in their personal studios. It is their personal space, where they are surrounded by their own work, which is inspirational.

Even with all the care taken to remove the objects of desire from our workplace, the thoughts may continue to raid our mind. We need to find a solution to that as well.

Meditation is a popular and effective way to quieten the mind, but the key is to retain this sense of quietude within. With sincere and regular efforts, we can rein in our thoughts and achieve mental peace.

Day 16

A yogi, who is in union with the Supreme Being, sees every being with an equal eye because of perceiving the omnipresent Spirit abiding in all beings and all beings abiding in the Supreme Being. (6.29)

A student of human anatomy will tell you that all human bodies look the same inside. The organs function the same way in everyone. This is to say, at a very gross level, that all humans are the same. They feel and suffer the same way, inside, unconsciously. The entire science of medicine is based on this premise.

At a finer level, we see that though people may feel the same way but they emote differently. This is at a conscious level, where the mind comes to play. Our behaviour is dictated by our mind, which in turn is affected by our upbringing, education and other environmental factors. Seeing this difference in behaviour, our mind starts judging people based on superficial parameters.

Mother Teresa said, 'If you judge people, you have no time to love them.' The wise do not discriminate. They are aware that all living beings carry the same life force, from the same source. Hence, the wise are always at peace with everyone.

Day 17

Those who perceive me in everything and behold everything in me, are not separated from me, and I am not separated from them. (6.30)

Little children are not concerned with the differences in people; they only look for similarities. When they play together, they don't see the racial differences; they just see that all of them seem to be somewhat of the same size. The children understand that they have common interests, like football or dance and so on—that is the reason for their bonding.

As they grow older, the parents and teachers start rewarding the children for their various achievements. This starts the idea of self-importance and ego.

In adults, it's the ego that creates all kinds of barriers among them. It's these barriers that create so much stress and unrest in the world. The only way to bring about harmony is to understand that no living being is different from the other. Life on this planet is a drama where everyone comes to play their part and then goes away.

When a person starts believing that everyone is equal, his ego disappears. Then it's easier to maintain a balanced mind. A balanced mind does not have any conflicts, and functions smoothly and peacefully.

Day 18

One is considered the best yogi who regards every being like oneself, and who can feel the pain and pleasures of others as one's own. (6.32)

Be it in governance or business, one who is compassionate and looks after others, keeping his own selfish interests aside, is considered to be an effective leader. When the leader looks after others selflessly, the others look after him by way of performing their best and achieving the collective goal.

Compassionate here does not mean emotional; it means considerate or thoughtful. People also confuse compassion with charity. They feel if they donate to some charity they have shown their compassion towards humankind. The same people may treat their employees harshly, deducting salaries in the name of discipline.

Forcing discipline does not work, compassion works. A wise leader knows this. He knows the strengths and shortcomings of his team and utilizes them in such a way that the result is a win-win for all.

Day 19

Undoubtedly, the mind is restless and difficult to restrain, but it is subdued by any constant vigorous spiritual practice such as meditation with perseverance, and by detachment. (6.35)

Affluence makes a person lazy. When we can afford to travel in a car, why would we walk then? It is the same with other things as well. We hire servants to pick things for us, to clean our surroundings and to cook for us.

The inevitable result of this kind of lifestyle is seen in our increasing weight. The body is not able to use up the food that we are putting into it, hence it starts storing it, in the form of fat. Excess weight results in all kinds of diseases, so we start exercising to push our lazy muscles into action.

It is the opposite with our mind. Ordinarily, the mind is very restless. In fact, the lazier the body, the more restless the mind becomes. It is always trying to discover more and more sensual pleasures for us, for our body.

Just as we need to exercise to bring our body into shape, similarly we need to meditate to bring our mind to rest. Physical activity done with persistence becomes a habit, so does meditation. We just need to set our goal and work towards it with dedication and detachment, and we shall succeed.

Day 20

There is no destruction for a yogi either here or hereafter. A transcendentalist is never put to grief. (6.40)

Something is better than nothing, as they say. Some action or some exercise is better than inaction or no exercise. A seed of an idea is better than no idea at all. This is to say that even if we have understood the fundamental truth of oneness of spiritual energy, it is good enough. The thought will take root and grow.

Detachment doesn't come overnight. We have to gradually start reigning in our sensory desires. Once they are in our control, only then can the mind function effectively.

In your workplace, you must have noticed that if phone calls or celebrating a colleague's birthday or anniversary, or even planning your next vacation, does not distract you, then you can achieve twice as much in a day. The solution normally is to tell your assistant not to let anyone disturb you till you finish your task at hand.

If we train our minds to not get distracted, then the phone calls will not bother us. Celebrations or anything else happening around us will not distract us. Distractions happen when we get involved emotionally. Emotional attachment here means thinking about the topic long after it is over. Detachment from emotional involvement makes our work smoother.

Day 21

The less evolved unsuccessful yogi is reborn in the house of the pious and prosperous after attaining heaven and living there for many years. The highly evolved successful yogi does not go to heaven, but is born in a spiritually advanced family. (6.41–6.42)

A man is known by the company he keeps, is a popular saying. It invariably happens that like-minded people gravitate towards each other. Right from childhood, we unconsciously make friends with those with whom we share common interests like sports or books.

Later on in college too, our close circle of friends comprises like-minded people. By now we become conscious of this fact. In workplace, we consciously seek out colleagues or even hire those who share a common interest with us. By now, of course, it is more professional than personal similarities that interest us.

This clearly shows that as we evolve mentally, our choices also evolve. We start shedding unnecessary or irrelevant attachments. In fact, we become more aware of our attachments or bonds. This awareness helps us to understand the truth and shed further material attachments as well. Finally, as we become detached, we attain eternal peace and happiness. This evolution happens at a different pace in different people.

Day 22

When he takes human form again in this world, he regains the knowledge acquired in his previous life and strives again to achieve perfection. (6.43)

Whatever we learn consciously or unconsciously never goes waste. We always manage to use it sometime or the other. When we join an organization as an assistant, we assist people in doing their jobs. Later on, as we grow in hierarchy in the workplace, we use what we had learnt as an assistant. And if we use it wisely, we rise higher in the chain of command. At some point of time, we actually are in a position to train an assistant.

This kind of growth is observed in most people in any workplace. At home too, what we learn from our parents, we pass on to our children, be it driving or cooking or any other life skills.

At a macro level, our soul, which is travelling from one form to the other over many lives, also carries with it the knowledge it acquires over those lifetimes. That is how it evolves. All knowledge is useful for our evolution, for our understanding of the basic truth of life. Once we have achieved that understanding, we attain freedom from the cycle of rebirths.

Day 23

The unsuccessful yogi is instinctively carried towards God by virtue of the impressions of yogic practices of previous lives. Even the inquirer of yoga surpasses those who perform Vedic rituals. (6.44)

Whether we want it or not, whether we like it or not, life goes on. Day will follow night as surely as winter is followed by summer. Everyone instinctively moves ahead.

Even if a person is not ambitious at work, they would still get their annual increments in salary and the bonus at the end of the year. In life too, they will continue to grow and evolve.

Awareness helps in speeding up the mental evolution. If we know our goal, we would make our path leading to it. We would learn whatever would be helpful in making our journey comfortable as well as expediting it. Otherwise, unaware, we would learn by committing mistakes on the way. Either way, we would eventually reach our goal.

The wise use their wisdom to detach themselves from the material world's trappings and reach their goal of peaceful bliss early in life.

Day 24

The yogi, who diligently strives, becomes completely free from all imperfections after gradually perfecting through many incarnations, and reaches the supreme abode. (6.45)

In Mahatma Gandhi's words, 'Life is an aspiration. Its mission is to strive after perfection, which is self-realization.'

If we set our heart to it, we can achieve anything. There are many rags-to-riches stories around us in the world. Larry Ellison was born in a slum, but managed to educate himself and ended up as the co-founder of Oracle.

Getting rid of attachments is a slow process and needs to be done diligently. Gradually, we start getting used to the freedom that breaking bonds brings with it. Our week starts better if we go off our computers over the weekend. But it's not easy. We have to be very firm with ourselves. Initially, such an action would cause anxiety. It is like withdrawal symptoms. But then, we would realize that it is de-stressing to switch off our machines at least once a week.

The material world makes us its slaves. We have entered the trap willingly. So, we should also get out of it willingly. Only then would this detachment last.

Once detached from worldly entanglements, we would reach the state of equanimity. The speed of our growth and evolution would escalate. We would taste success earlier than our peers, as with no attachments the journey becomes smoother and faster.

Day 25

The yogi, who is devoted to meditation, is superior to the ascetics. The yogi is superior to the Vedic scholars. The yogi is superior to the ritualists. Therefore, be a yogi. (6.46)

Wealthy industrialists eventually start taking interest in philanthropy. Once they have more than enough for themselves and their children, they realize that maybe they should share with those who are less fortunate. Charity as a ritual to feel good about your own self is not real charity. It has to be done from your heart. You have to understand the need of the person who is receiving and not your own need to give.

Likewise, reading scriptures or listening to sermons from holy people is not going to make us holy. Reading books can only teach us the theory; we need to practise what we have learnt to understand it better. We must visit the Taj Mahal personally to see and understand its beauty; reading about it cannot suffice.

Meditation is a part of yoga, where we become aware of our own breath and understand that the same universal Spirit flows through all living beings. This practical understanding sets us free from all material attachments.

Day 26

I consider the yogi-devotee who lovingly contemplates on me with supreme faith, and whose mind is ever absorbed in me, to be the best of all the yogis. (6.47)

Yoga is defined as the union of our soul with the universal energy source, or God, as it's called by some. It is achieved by focussing on the source and stilling the mind.

These days, more so than before, doctors also prescribe meditation. It helps the mind to relax and focus on getting well. Otherwise, with Google's availability on every smartphone, the patients fill themselves up with a lot of misinformation and fall sicker.

Meditation teaches us to focus on one point. And in doing so, while observing the movement of our own breath, our thoughts fall away. This should be the state of our mind at all times. It's an ideal state where, unfettered by worldly attachments, we move on towards eternal peace.

When we observe the flow of our own breath, we realize it's the same breath that flows through every living being. And once we understand that, we treat all living beings the same way. This is real yoga.

7

Knowledge of the Ultimate Truth

27 May–12 June

Day 27

The mind, intellect, ego, ether, air, fire, water and earth are the eightfold divisions of my nature. (7.04)

The supernatural power or the cosmic energy is the source of all living beings. This fact has been established already. According to the scriptures, the entire creation is made up of five basic elements in different proportions. The elements are earth, water, fire, air and space or ether.

All solid matter has more of earth element; all liquids have more of water. Fire transforms one state of matter into another. Air is everything gaseous. Ether is the subtlest of all elements and carries radio frequencies, light and other cosmic rays.

Nature requires that these elements remain in a balanced state, as their imbalance causes diseases. Yoga helps to maintain their balance. Other than these, mind, reasoning or intellect and ego are three more elements that are present in a human being.

As everything else, the five basic natural and the three subtle elements are also the manifestation of God or the universal cosmic energy.

Day 28

The material nature or matter is my lower nature. My higher nature is the Spirit by which this entire universe is sustained. (7.05)

There are two kinds of nature of God, the first one is matter or material, which is his lower nature. The second or the higher nature is the Spirit, without which the matter remains inert.

Matter, also known as prakriti, is inert, insentient, while the indwelling Spirit, also known as purush, is sentient, dynamic. A combination of matter and Spirit causes things to be born and function.

In a steam engine, the iron and steel components cannot function without steam passing through them. The engine is matter and the steam is the Spirit-factor. Only when they unite can we say that a steam engine is created. It is the Spirit that makes an inert acorn to grow into a mighty oak tree.

Once we understand the difference between matter and Spirit, we realize that the cause of all our suffering is due to the Spirit identifying with matter. When we detach the Spirit from all its identifications, it realizes its original nature of bliss.

Day 29

Know that all creatures have evolved from this twofold energy; and the Supreme Spirit is the source of origin as well as dissolution of the entire universe. (7.06)

We have already seen that the higher and lower natures together cause the manifestation of the world. If there is no matter, the dynamic Spirit would not have any field to express itself. Matter is dormant and cannot function till the Spirit activates or enlivens it.

Like in the case of electricity and bulb, both are of no use till they get together. Electricity here is the dynamic Spirit-factor that enlivens the bulb, which is the inert matter.

In every case, we find that the presence and absence of Spirit is the cause of life and death of matter, respectively. Matter or prakriti on its own cannot generate anything. The Spirit, therefore, is the cause of creation and dissolution of the universe. But then, someone has to direct what to create and what to dissolve. That power is called the Supreme Being or God.

So it boils down to God deciding to put the Spirit or consciousness into matter resulting in the creation of the universe or taking the Spirit away from matter resulting in the dissolution of the universe.

Day 30

There is nothing higher than the Supreme Being. Everything in the universe is strung on the Supreme Being, like jewels are strung on the thread of a necklace. (7.07)

We have already seen that God or the Supreme Being is the cause of the creation of the universe. He is also the supporter of the entire universe. Just like the string supports the different beads strung together with it in a necklace, so does God support all living beings in the universe.

There is a huge variety of living beings in the universe but all carry the same universal Spirit. It is like a variety of beads, all of different materials, strung together by one single string made of an entirely different material.

Just like the Spirit, though, we cannot see the string hidden in the beads, we are aware of its existence and importance in the necklace. When the string breaks, the beads fall apart and the necklace ceases to exist. Likewise, without the Spirit, the universe would cease to exist.

At the micro level too, in our body, the various organs coexist and function in harmony because of the life force or Spirit running through them.

Day 31

I am the sapidity in the water, I am the radiance in the sun and the moon, the sacred syllable AUM in all the vedas, the sound in the ether and potency in human beings. I am the sweet fragrance in the earth. I am the heat in the fire, the life in all living beings and the austerity in the ascetics. (7.08–7.09)

Everything in this universe is different; no two leaves, no two snowflakes or no two fingerprints are the same. We can safely claim that everything is unique.

That which remains from beginning to end, without which the thing cannot be identified, is its essence. Like the taste of pure water, the radiance of the sun and the moon, the heat of fire, the fragrance of earth and flowers—they are special to them, they are the active principle, the essence. This pure, uncontaminated, unexplained essence is present due to the Supreme Being or God or Krishna.

When an artist creates a painting, he knows exactly which paint and how much of it is to be used where. He also knows what he has to draw; he is aware of every square inch of his canvas. So is God; he has created this universe as one huge live painting or a film. He is the cause of everything that exists in that film. God is like the light beaming from the projection room on to the screen, creating the film—one beam of light resulting in so many singing, dancing characters.

JUNE

Day 1

Know me to be the eternal seed of all creatures. I am the intelligence of the intelligent, and the brilliance of the brilliant. I am the strength of the strong who is devoid of selfish attachment. I am the lust in human beings that is devoid of sense gratification and is in accord with dharma. (7.10–7.11)

God is not only the eternal seed-cause of the entire creation, but also the intelligence of a person, because without intelligence one cannot understand the eternal truth. He is also the strength of the strong the strength to protect the weak, not to oppress them. But all these qualities are without desire or attachment.

Desire is for what is absent in our lives and attachment is for what we have already obtained or achieved. These two emotions are the root cause of most conflicts, be it between individuals, families, communities or countries.

But here Krishna clarifies that lust or desire is not bad if it is devoid of sense gratification. All thoughts or actions entertained by a person, which are in accordance to dharma, are righteous. For instance, sex for the purpose of procreation or propagating life is not wrong. So, God is in all those desires that are not wrongful to a living being.

Day 2

Know that three modes of material nature—goodness, passion and ignorance—also emanate from me. I am not dependent on or affected by the modes of material nature, but the modes of material nature are dependent on me. (7.12)

We have seen that God is manifested as purush or soul or consciousness and prakriti or nature or matter. Prakriti has three modes or gunas, namely sattva, rajas and tamas.

Sattva denotes goodness or serenity and harmony, rajas denotes passion or restlessness and tamas denotes ignorance or inertia. Everything in nature is made of these three modes in varying measures.

Material nature or prakriti is a manifestation of God and hence is dependent on him, though God himself is independent of it. It is like the king, who is the lawmaker of his own kingdom, is himself not subject to the laws that he has created; like the ocean, which is not affected by the waves that it creates, while the waves certainly are affected by it.

God has created us in his image. And as he is not affected by the cosmic delusion of the three modes of material nature, so should we strive to remain unaffected by the material world around us.

Day 3

Human beings are deluded by various aspects of these three modes of material nature; therefore, they do not know me, who is eternal and above these modes. (7.13)

The three modes of nature give rise to all the emotions like love, hatred, anger, envy, etc., and these emotions create attachments. We get trapped in the worldly attachments and are unable to see God as the cause behind everything.

It is like when we are watching a film in a theatre. We do not pay attention to the beam of light which is being projected from the projection room on to the screen in front of us, resulting in the film that we are enjoying. We are totally engrossed and lost in what we are watching on the screen. Till the time the film is running, we continue being lost in it.

Likewise, in life we are so wrapped up in gratifying our senses, that we do not realize that our soul remains unchanged and unaffected all through the stages of our growth, sickness and decay, till death. In the end, the soul moves on, leaving this physical body behind.

Day 4

This divine power (maya) of mine, consisting of three states of matter or mind, is very difficult to overcome. Only those who surrender unto me easily cross over this maya. (7.14)

Since the universal soul and the material nature, both emanate from God, both are considered divine. The three states of matter or mind, namely serenity, restlessness and ignorance, are also divine by the same definition. So the problem is not in the material states but is in getting trapped by them.

When we go to any shopping mall, we see many shops, each selling hundreds of products. We don't have to buy all of them. In fact, we need not buy any. The products, their sellers, would continue to lure us with all kinds of offers. And we may succumb and end up buying something or the other.

Our senses keep pulling us in different directions and we continue to get enmeshed deeper and deeper in the sensory world. This is the problem. To get out of this problem, we need to find the origin of it.

When hypnotists hypnotize someone, they can get them to do or feel anything that they want. The only way to get out of this situation is when the hypnotists themselves snap their fingers to release the person from hypnosis. So, it stands to reason that since the delusory material world is created by God, the way out of it is also with him.

Day 5

Four types of virtuous ones worship or seek me. They are: the distressed, the seeker of Self-knowledge, the seeker of wealth, and the enlightened one who has experienced the Supreme Being. (7.16)

Why do we pray? By praying we are trying to reach God or whatever superpower we believe in. We assume that the superpower is listening and would answer, somehow.

When do we pray? We pray mostly when we are in trouble, when we reach a dead end with our problem and have no answers. That is the time we pray to God or the superpower and seek answers. Like when a loved one is very sick, we pray for them to get well; when we want to get admission in a college or get the job we desire, we pray to God to fulfil our desires. This is a distress situation.

However, there are people who pray to seek wisdom in order to realize their own divinity and to understand the mystery of life. Here also there are unanswered questions, but then it's not a distress situation.

The third case is of those who pray to seek wealth and power in this life and thereafter. They want the best of both the worlds, so no distress here. The fourth type are those who want nothing; they pray out of love and respect for God. They are the wisest of all.

Day 6

All these seekers are indeed noble. But, I regard the enlightened devotee as my very Self, because the one who is steadfast abides in my Supreme Abode. (7.18)

The very fact that a person has recognized or accepted the presence of a superpower or God is the first step towards attaining everlasting peace. When we accept that there is a superpower controlling us and everything around us, then we can begin to move in its direction. Hence, all the devotees are noble, according to Krishna.

At the micro level, the devotees who pray unconditionally are superior to those who have reasons or some hidden agenda for praying. When people pray for a reason, they are expecting favourable results. They are attached to the fruit of their action.

The path of prayer is right, but in order to attain eternal peace and happiness, we need to detach ourselves from any fruit of any of our actions. The ones who indulge in selfless prayer are enlightened beings. They are closest to the supreme power or God as they have understood the universal truth. They have realized that they, as well as all the other living beings, are a part of the same universal soul. They have realized the God in themselves.

Day 7

After many births, the enlightened one resorts to me by realizing that everything is, indeed, my (or Supreme Being's) manifestation. Such a great soul is very rare. (7.19)

We live in the midst of a material world, surrounded by temptations. Our life is spent in fulfilling our desires, as our five senses keep pushing and pulling us in different directions. Whatever we are unable to achieve in this life, we carry those desires with us to the next life. Like this, we keep taking birth to realize our unfulfilled dreams.

The karmic cycle of rebirth can go on forever, which it does for some souls. But there are some people who realize the futility of such a life. They are able to break free from this cycle of bondage by detaching themselves from all material attachments.

These wise people are able to see that the entire universe is a manifestation of the superpower or God. Such people are able to keep their senses in check and live a life of selfless service.

Once we realize this truth, our attachments disappear; we have no need to take birth again to fulfil any leftover desires, as there are none left. We successfully break away from the cycle of rebirth.

Day 8

Whosoever desires to worship whatever deity—using any name, form, and method— with faith, I make their faith steady in that very deity. Endowed with steady faith they worship that deity and obtain their wishes through that deity. Those wishes are granted by me. (7.21–7.22)

Faith here means absolute belief in the existence of divine or superpower. Faith brings success to worship. In Dr S. Radhakrishnan's words, 'All worship elevates. No matter what we revere, so long as our reverence is serious, it helps progress.'

In India we pray to different gods for different reasons, for example, Sarasvati is considered the goddess of learning and Lakshmi, the goddess of wealth. So, people pray according to the need of the hour. When people are in trouble due to their enemies, they pray to Hanuman and when they are sick they pray to Surya.

But we know that the entire creation has one source, which is the universal consciousness. This applies to the various gods and goddesses as well. They are names or manifestations of the different aspects of the universal consciousness or God.

So when we pray to one goddess or god, we are actually praying to one particular aspect of the main God. Hence, whatever we wish for, is granted by the universal consciousness itself.

Day 9

The ignorant ones, unable to understand my immutable, incomparable, incomprehensible and transcendental form, assume that I, the Supreme Being, am formless and take forms or incarnate. Concealed by my divine power (maya), I do not reveal myself to such deluded ones. (7.24–7.25)

The unseen water vapour can be condensed into water and frozen into ice. Similarly, the impersonal God can be projected into any form of the devotee's liking and worshipped as a finite personality. However, the devotee would be foolish if he limits his understanding of God to that finite form.

Even Sri Ramakrishna Paramhansa did the same initially. Later he said, 'I had to destroy the finite form of Ma Kali with the sword of wisdom, to behold her as the formless infinite.'[2]

Our minds are perpetually agitated by thoughts that emanate from the five senses in the form of desires and emotions. It is these desires and emotions that lead us to singular, limited deities to pray

---

[2] Swami Kriyananda, *Paramhansa Yogananda A Biography*, Ananda Sangha, 2011.

to, for the fulfilment of our desires. Once our desire is fulfilled, we are convinced of the power of the deity and forget the omnipresent nature of the universal consciousness that is also present in the deity as well as everything else, including our own selves.

Only by self-control, reflection and meditation can we quieten and control the agitations of our mind and discover the universal consciousness within.

Day 10

All beings in this world are in utter ignorance due to delusion of pairs of opposites born of likes and dislikes. But persons of unselfish deeds, whose karma or sin has come to an end, become free from the delusion of pairs of opposites and worship me with firm resolve. (7.27–7.28)

Since all of us are going through cycles of rebirth, we are born with leftover desires from our past life. Our current life is usually spent in fulfilling those desires. While doing so, we get trapped in more desires, since the world we live in is full of temptations.

The result is that we are always going through the pair of opposites: like-dislike, love-hate. We like to possess something, for example a laptop, but because of certain family circumstances we are unable to buy it. This leads to our hating those circumstances or the people responsible for those circumstances. This conflict between desire and aversion goes on right throughout our lives. Our intellect is perpetually occupied either chasing the object of our desire or running away from the object of our aversion.

The wise are in control of their senses. They cannot fall into this trap of opposites as they remain detached from the material world. Such people pray to God selflessly and achieve eternal peace and happiness.

Day 11

Those who strive for freedom from the cycles of birth, old age and death—by taking refuge in God—fully comprehend the true nature and powers of the Supreme. (7.29)

Birth, growth, disease, decay and death are the normal processes that any living being goes through. The thing to remember here is that all this happens to the physical body, while the soul residing in the body remains untouched.

Practically, no one can be free from their body's ageing process. The freedom mentioned here is the freedom from attachment to the body and the bodily processes. When we identify with our body, we get attached to it and are upset by anything affecting it. We are scared by the mere thought of losing our body one day.

The wise understand the nature and power of the universal soul that is within us. They know that the soul remains untouched and moves on from one body to the next. When this realization is there, where is the need or use of any attachment to the material world?

The material world is ever-changing and perishable whereas the soul is eternal. Comprehension of this truth releases us from all mental bondages.

Day 12

The wise ones, who know me alone as the basis of all the mortal beings, Temporal Being and the Eternal Being even at the time of death, attain me. (7.30)

It is not easy for us to ignore the world in which we are living. Right from our childhood we get used to facing competition, be it in studies or sports. As we grow older, we start competing with our colleagues in the race for promotions. Then there are relatives and neighbours, family and friends, who egg us to continuously upgrade ourselves.

Do we ever stop to consider why we are always running a race? When no two persons can be the same, no two circumstances can be the same, then why compete? The most important question to ask is, where is the finishing line of this race that we are running?

The wise know that the same universal soul is present in every living being. Since we all are a part of one supreme energy, whom are we competing against?

But then, knowledge of anything is useless if it is not put to practical use. We need to apply the understanding of the cosmic truth in our lives. We have to be in control of our senses and remain detached from the material world. This does not mean that we need to leave our home. We can fulfil our duties selflessly even while living in the material world, if we remain detached from it. Just like a lotus grows and blooms in muddy waters without getting soiled, so can we remain free from all attachments.

Being in such a state at all times, right till their death, the wise achieve eternal peace. Such beings do not need to be born again as mortals, as they have no desires to fulfil.

8

Attainment of Salvation

13 June–1 July

Day 13

The eternal and immutable Spirit of the Supreme Being is also called Eternal Being or the Spirit. The inherent power of cognition and desire of the Spirit is called the nature of the Eternal Being. The creative power of the Spirit that causes manifestation of the living entity is called karma. (8.03)

Krishna talks about three things here—the indestructible Spirit, the soul, the unfulfilled desires that it carries and its manifestation as a living entity.

What we see physically is the result of karma. The living beings are born because of their karma, their unfulfilled desires. The soul is the essence of a living being. Though it is the same in all beings, yet the soul identifies with the being that it inhabits and behaves in relation to the desires it carries from the past life. This behaviour constitutes its nature.

The soul may keep changing its behaviour, but one thing constant in the entire creation, the entire universe, is the universal consciousness or the Spirit. It is this Spirit, also addressed as God or Krishna, which illumines our body, mind and soul. It is like light, without which we cannot see anything.

Day 14

There are various expansions of the Supreme Being. That which underlies all the elements and is the basis of physical existence, is the perishable entity or adhibhoota. That which underlies all the devtaas and is the basis of astral existence, is the cosmic entity or adhidaiva. The Supreme Being also resides inside the physical bodies as the Divine Controller or adhiyajna. (8.04)

The physical nature is always changing. Anything that is born would always grow, produce by-products, dwindle and finally die. This perishable existence is called adhibhoota.

The presiding deities of the five senses, mind and intellect are the adhidaiva. The planets and their deities or demigods are also adhidaiva.

Present in the body, along with the individual soul, is the super-soul, the Spirit or Krishna or just God. The individual soul is called atma and the super-soul is called paramatma or adhiyajna. Seated next to the individual soul in the heart, the super-soul is a witness to all its activities and, hence, is also called antaryami.

Existing in the cosmos as the originating and governing intelligence and in the human body as soul, the Spirit or super-soul, therefore, is the creative underlying substance of the physical, astral and causal universes with their various kinds of beings. The wise are aware of this play of the Spirit at the physical, mental and intellectual levels.

Day 15

The one who remembers the Supreme Being exclusively even while leaving the body at the time of death, attains the Supreme Abode; there is no doubt about it. (8.05)

All our waking moments in life are spent working towards fulfilling our desires, which are many and never-ending. All the desires are created by our senses. We want to eat a variety of tasteful delicacies, we want to wear the finest of clothes and jewellery, we want to use the best of perfumes, we want to travel and see beautiful places around the world, we want to possess the most advanced gadgets to smoothen our daily life and the list goes on.

As with everything, the desires are also part of our habits. We are told as children to set our goals in life and work hard towards achieving them; this becomes our habit as we grow up. We create many short-term goals of achieving happiness through material objects. Without realizing it, we get trapped in the web of the material world.

By practising yoga and meditation, we can learn to control our senses. Once the senses are controlled, it is not difficult to detach ourselves from the material world. It's just a matter of inculcating a new habit—the habit of saying 'no' to temptations.

We know that our soul returns to fulfil our unfulfilled desires; it stands to reason that if we are desireless, the soul would not return. We would break away from the cycle of rebirth. Our soul would then merge with its source, the Supreme Being.

Day 16

Remembering whatever object at the end of life while one leaves the body, one attains that object. Thought of whatever object prevails during one's lifetime, one remembers only that object at the end of life and achieves it. (8.06)

The most recurring thought of our life becomes the most prominent one at the time of our death. And our last thought determines our soul's next birth. What we think we become. Our past thoughts have determined our present and our present thoughts would determine our future.

The point to remember here is that it's not just the last thought at the time of death but the persistent thought all through our life that determines the soul's next destination.

Some people feel guilty for their misdeeds, some are constantly hankering after wealth, while some regret not having spent time with their loved ones and some dream of travelling across the world to see exotic places. Whatever the feeling, it is the determining cause that leads the soul to another incarnation on earth, in order to seek closure.

When we practise yoga and meditation, we realize how meaningless our desires are and how mechanical our life is. This realization creates detachment and all our desires vanish. We become free.

Day 17

Therefore, always remember me and do your duty. You shall certainly attain me if your mind and intellect are ever focused on me. (8.07)

Considering that what we think in our heart, so we become, the next step logically would be to contemplate on the super-soul or the Supreme Being. And since we are contemplating on the super-soul or God, our soul would merge with it after it leaves our mortal body.

Sounds easy, but that is not what Krishna advised Arjun. Krishna told Arjun not to give up his prescribed duties to contemplate on God. He should continue performing his tasks but also think of God.

When we are performing any task, we tend to think about its result, desiring a positive outcome. We do not realize that the results cannot be controlled by us, as there could be multiple factors involved. For instance, when Arjun was fighting, he could only hope for his weapons to kill his enemies, but could he guarantee that?

Krishna's advice to Arjun was to work selflessly, without worrying about the result. And in this detached state of mind, he should think about God, the super-soul, as everything happened only according to his will. So, even if Arjun died while fighting, since he would be contemplating on God, his soul would merge with the super-soul.

Day 18

One who meditates on the Supreme Being as the omniscient, the oldest, the controller, smaller than the smallest and bigger than the biggest, the sustainer of everything, the inconceivable, the self-luminous like the sun, and transcendental at the time of death, with steadfast mind and devotion, attains the Supreme Being. (8.09–8.10)

The Supreme Being or God, or Krishna in this case, is omniscient. He is the knower of everything. No knowledge is possible without him. He is the oldest, because he was present before the creation; he is the creator of the creation.

In order to lead a meaningful existence, our physical, mental and intellectual processes have to be in harmony. Apart from achieving inner harmony, we have to be in tune with the world around us as well. This would not be possible if we didn't have the principle of awareness present in our faculties of perception, feeling and comprehension. This principle of awareness is the Super Consciousness or essence of life. Just as clay is the essence of a clay pot, so is the Super Consciousness or Supreme Being the essence or controller of the universe.

We have seen that the Super Consciousness is present in and sustains everything, the smallest of the small and the largest of the large. It means that it is smaller than the smallest, in order to pervade it. Likewise, it is bigger than the biggest, in order to sustain it. The Supreme Being is infinite, hence inconceivable.

Though the Supreme Being may be beyond our comprehension, yet it can be experienced. The wise, the enlightened beings, can understand it to be their own Self, their own super-soul.

Day 19

When one leaves the physical body by controlling all the senses, focusing the life-breath between the eyebrows, meditating on me and uttering

AUM, the sacred monosyllable sound power of Spirit, one attains the Supreme Abode. (8.12–8.13)

The five sense organs, eyes, ears, nose, tongue and skin are the entry points through which the external stimuli reach the mind and cause agitations in it. These senses have to be controlled by using the discriminatory powers of the mind, which would result in detachment. Yoga helps in doing that.

Although external stimuli can be avoided by controlling the senses, there is always a possibility for the mind to get disturbed by memories of the past. What do you do about that? Meditation helps us to focus on our life-breath and stilling the mind.

When we reach the state of physical, mental and intellectual equipoise, then focussing our life-breath between our eyebrows, chanting AUM, contemplating on the super-soul, we get connected to it. When our soul leaves our body at this moment, it merges with its source, the super-soul.

Day 20

I am easily attainable by that ever steadfast devotee who always thinks of me and whose mind does not go elsewhere. (8.14)

The law of attraction operates at all levels for everyone everywhere. According to this law, our thoughts and energy can create our reality. And we use this law unknowingly all the time.

We set our goals in life, like getting a job of our liking, having a house of our own, marrying the right person and so on. One by one we go about achieving these goals with a clear focus and positive attitude.

But then, life is long and the ever-changing goals of material achievements start telling on our mental and physical health. This is the time when we pause and reflect. We realize that we have created too many goals to achieve, like a bigger house to live in and another one to rent out, a bigger vehicle and maybe a vehicle for each member of our growing family, the list is never-ending. Somewhere along the way, we switched tracks from desiring necessities to desiring luxuries. We continued looking for happiness, but in the wrong place.

Once we understand what happiness really means and that the perishable material world provides perishable happiness, we change our focus to imperishable eternal happiness. The source of such happiness is in the opposite direction—in detachment from the material world. Freeing ourselves from material attachments, we become focussed on the supreme creator, the universal energy, God. This is the path to eternal peace and happiness.

Day 21

After attaining me, the great souls do not incur rebirth in this miserable transitory world, because they have attained the highest perfection. (8.15)

Looking around us, we see so much misery and pain. It is not limited to those who are poor or sick, it applies to everyone. Those who have amassed a great deal of wealth are also miserable. They constantly worry about how to keep themselves and their wealth safe. With so much money at their disposal, they want to live forever and spend a fortune to maintain their youthful looks. They forget that their bodies are growing old from inside.

The stress of maintaining their lifestyle takes a toll on their health. Even getting the best of treatments cannot prolong their lives beyond a point. Even on their deathbed, they are worried about what would happen to their wealth. Without realizing it, such people have been miserable for most of their lives.

The souls that have managed to detach themselves from this world of miseries do not incur rebirth. They are desireless; they are free; they do not need to start the cycle of rebirth again.

Day 22

The dwellers of all the worlds, up to and including the world of the creator, are subject to the miseries of repeated birth and death. But, after attaining me, one does not take birth again. (8.16)

The Hindu scriptures are full of stories about gods living up there in heaven and demons living below in hell. We, the humans, live on earth, in between. The stories revolve around the interactions among the inhabitants of these three realms.

In these stories, there are gods who fall prey to greed or anger and indulge in wrong actions, resulting in their being born again to rectify their mistakes. There are stories of demons who are so good that they are born again in heaven as a reward. The idea behind these stories is to show—as you sow, so shall you reap.

The stories also tell us that no one is exempted from the cycle of rebirth. The only way out is to understand the cosmic truth and follow it in our lives. In the detached, desireless state we realize God within us. There's no coming back after this.

Day 23

Those who know that the duration of creation lasts for billions of years and that the duration of destruction also lasts for billions of years, they are the knowers of the cycles of creation and destruction. (8.17)

Krishna wants Arjun to realize how insignificant man's existence is in the larger scheme of things.

According to the Hindu scriptures, Lord Brahma is the first manifestation of the Supreme Spirit. From him were created the rest of the beings, hence he is also called the creator of the universe, though the original creator is the Spirit.

The entire period of cosmic manifestation or evolution is known as the day of Brahma, while the period of destruction or dissolution is his night. So, as can be seen, the duration of the material universe is limited.

The substance, a cloud-like darkness, from which the material world is created is called the causal ocean. In this ocean are several Brahmas, rising and disappearing like bubbles. Each Brahma manages his own universe. Even Brahma is not spared from the cycle of birth and death, though he is engaged in the service of the Supreme Spirit in the management of the material universe.

The wise know their own insignificance in the universe and hence remain detached from it.

Day 24

All manifestations come out of the primary material nature during the creative cycle, and they merge into the primary material nature during the destructive cycle. The same multitude of beings come into existence again and again at the arrival of the creative cycle and are annihilated, inevitably, at the arrival of the destructive cycle. (8.18-19)

All of us, who are attached to this material world, continue to be born again. We keep shunting back and forth in between the realms of heaven, earth and hell, depending on our karma and material desires.

This happens during Brahma's day which, as mentioned earlier, is thousands of years long. So we, or rather our soul, keeps shunting for thousands of years like this. When Brahma's day ends and night begins, all souls, including ours, get annihilated. This is another long period of thousands of years.

After a long night, the day comes again and the cycle of rebirth begins, and so on and so forth. Ultimately, when Brahma's life is finished, all souls are annihilated and remain unborn for millions of years. When Brahma is born again in another millennium, the souls are reborn to start off yet another round of births and deaths.

Day 25

There is another eternal transcendental existence higher than the changeable material nature called Eternal Being or Spirit that does not perish when all created beings perish. This is also called the Supreme Abode. Those who attain the Supreme Abode do not take birth again. (8.20-21)

As mentioned earlier, Brahma was the first manifestation of the super-soul or the Spirit. This was done to facilitate creation. It is like when the owner or promoter of a company sets up his first company, he installs a managing director to run it. Meanwhile, he sets up more companies.

The Spirit or the Eternal Being, whom we address as God or Krishna, is also the owner or controller of the universe that he creates. He himself is eternal and imperishable, while his creation is transient and perishable.

The Spirit is like a mass or an ocean of energy, from where the creation emanates and into which it dissolves back. Just like the bubbles in water or waves in the ocean, the energy mass remains constant, undisturbed and unchanged, while the bubbles or waves come and go.

The souls that escape the cycle of rebirth remain in the causal ocean as part of the universal energy or Spirit.

Day 26

This Supreme Abode is attainable by unswerving devotion to me within which all beings exist, and by which the entire universe is pervaded. (8.22)

Just as the essential nature of a clay pot is nothing but the clay with which it's made, so is the essential nature of all beings in the world the same as the Spirit from where they emanate.

Yoga and meditation teach us to concentrate on our breath,

resulting in stilling the mind. In this journey inwards, we realize soon enough that all attachments to thoughts, people and things are useless, as everything is transitory, perishable. Since we know that we cannot carry our wealth with us when we die, we don't mind using it to help the needy.

When the realization dawns that all living beings are a part of the same universal soul, that we are made of the same energy, all forms of discrimination drop from our system. We become happier and at peace. This also results in our indulging in selfless service. This, according to Krishna, is unswerving devotion to God or the universal soul.

Day 27

Fire, light, daytime, the bright lunar fortnight and the six months of the northern solstice of the sun—departing by the paths of these celestial controllers, yogis who know the Spirit attain the Supreme. (8.24)

Krishna says that the path to liberation from the cycle of rebirths is the way of light or path of fire. Fire here means life energy. Yoga teaches us how to control our life-breath or life-energy and, through meditation, we learn to focus between our eyebrows. This is the site of the divine eye which, when activated, enlightens us and makes us realize the cosmic truth.

Daytime indicates the awakening of the person. When the divine eye opens, it's like the light switching on, dispelling the darkness. When the person understands the cosmic truth, all the darkness of confusion disappears from his brain, hence the term enlightened.

The moon doesn't have its own light, it reflects that of the sun, waxing and waning for a fortnight each in a month. Since the enlightened person is reflecting the light of the universal soul, he is compared to the bright lunar fortnight of the waxing moon.

Finally, the six months of the northern course of the sun indicate the six spinal centres starting from the base of the spine to the brain. This is the path of consciousness. Yoga helps our consciousness follow the path to enlightenment or attaining the Supreme.

Day 28

Smoke, night, the dark lunar fortnight and the six months of southern solstice of the sun—departing by these paths, the righteous person attains heaven and comes back to earth. (8.25)

Krishna explains the path of darkness here, which leads to the continued cycle of rebirths.

Smoke means ignorance or delusion that results in our increasing attachment to the material world. When this smoke of delusion obscures the divine eye, the darkness caused thereby is referred to as night.

The dark lunar fortnight is when the moon wanes and becomes smaller and smaller till it disappears completely. It can also be looked at as a light diminishing slowly. This denotes the person's increasing entrapment in the sensory material world. Such a soul keeps getting reborn to fulfil its never-ending desires. The births cannot end till the desires don't end.

Day 29

The path of light of spiritual practice and Self-knowledge and the path of darkness of materialism and ignorance are thought to be the world's two eternal paths. The former leads to salvation and the latter leads to rebirth as human beings. (8.26)

Life is a constant conflict between the right and wrong paths. All the religious texts, scriptures, mythology and folklore across the world tell us stories about this conflict. In every story, the end is predictable; the hero wins or the good wins over the evil. And when that happens, it becomes a cause for celebration and, more often than not, results in the birth of a festival.

Though there might be many stories where the good doesn't win in the end, but somehow, they are not as satisfying as the traditional 'happy endings'. Why? This is because we are born to naturally seek happiness, which we do consciously and unconsciously.

Though there can be endless debates over what is good for one may not be good for another, the fact remains that light and darkness are the same for all. Hence, Krishna mentioned the way of light and the way of darkness being the only two paths in front of us.

Light is that of knowledge, not academic but spiritual. It is the knowledge of our own self, our soul and super-soul. This knowledge cannot come from studying scriptures alone, it comes from understanding the cosmic truth and realizing the God within us. Ignorance and materialism lead to the path of darkness, which is the path of rebirths in the mortal world.

Day 30

Knowing these two paths, a yogi is not bewildered at all. Therefore, one should be resolute in attaining salvation as the goal of human birth, at all times. (8.27)

The wise are aware of their choices of the two paths and they naturally choose the path of light.

In fact, the very realization that we live in a material world, which is full of temptations to confuse and trap us, is the first glimpse of light. This understanding takes us further on the path of light, away from all the delusions. The wise also realize that in order to escape the material world, one has to control one's senses and drop all attachments.

In showing these two paths, Krishna is telling Arjun that while performing his worldly duties he should constantly remain in touch with God, as that is the path of light. It is the aim of each soul to return to its source, the universal soul, and the path of light leads to it.

JULY

Day 1

The one who knows all this knowledge goes beyond getting the benefits of the study of the vedas, performance of sacrifices, austerities, charities and salvation. (8.28)

According to the vedas, human life should be divided into four stages. The first 25 years should be spent in studying in isolation, away from all temptations. After becoming proficient in whatever field or subject, the person should spend the next 25 years using that proficiency to earn a living, get married and raise a family.

The next 25 years should be spent in living a retired life after winding up the household responsibilities. In the earlier phase, one was bogged down by so many family duties, but in this phase of life one is free to travel. Here travel means inward as well as outward. Inward travelling or introspection is crucial to evaluate one's life and learn lessons from it. The fourth or the last 25 years should be spent in detaching oneself from any material attachments. Control of senses and detachment from the material world leads one towards enlightenment.

The wise cut the process short. With the help of yoga and meditation, they control their senses and drop all attachments. Consequently, they reach the stage of enlightenment very early in life, after which they continue leading their lives working selflessly. Whenever their soul decides to leave their body, it merges straight away with its source, the super-soul.

9

Secret of Supreme Knowledge

2–26 July

Day 2

Self-knowledge is the king of all knowledge, is the most secret, is very sacred; it can be perceived by instinct, conforms to righteousness (dharma), is very easy to practise and is timeless. (9.02)

Enlightenment or Self-knowledge that we have been talking about is true wisdom according to Krishna; it is the king of all knowledge.

The other subjects like philosophy, biology, chemistry, physics, astronomy, mathematics, geography, etc., teach us about everything in the world, but none teach us about the Spirit or the soul. Without soul our body is useless, yet people give importance to the necessities of the body rather than that of the soul.

Knowledge of Self cannot be acquired from books or teachers; it has to be experienced. And once experienced it is never forgotten. 'Most secret' implies how deeply embedded it is within us. After all, it is our core! Once the veils of delusion are lifted, we experience the cosmic truth, we experience our Self. This process of perception is instinctive.

People believe that God is elusive and unknowable, Krishna says otherwise. God is universal consciousness, the super-soul present in all beings. Knowledge of Self is the same as knowing God. God is eternal and timeless, so is Self-knowledge.

Day 3

Those who have no faith in this knowledge do not attain me, and follow the cycles of birth and death. (9.03)

Faith is complete trust or confidence in something or someone. Faith can move mountains, they say. We may not realize it but our day to day life is based on faith. We have faith in our parents as our children have in us; how else can any relationship survive? When we fall sick we go to a doctor with the faith that he would cure our sickness. It's with great faith in the education system that we send our children to school or college.

In today's language, one can say that faith is like Wi-Fi; it is invisible but has the power to connect us with what we need. In Mahatma Gandhi's words, 'Faith is nothing but a living, wide-awake consciousness of God within. He who has achieved that faith wants nothing.'

Unfortunately, most of us tend to have faith only in things that our senses can recognize, something that we have read or heard about. Such conditional faith would continue to lead us on the path of rebirths.

Day 4

This entire universe is an expansion of mine. All beings depend on me like a chain depends on gold, and the milk products depend on milk. I do not depend on or am affected by them; because I am the highest of all. (9.04)

We are aware that the entire universe is created by the union of purush and prakriti. The one who is making this union happen is the Supreme Power or God. Not only does he create and control the entire creation, he is also present in everything that is created.

A simple example can be of air, which is invisible and is all around us. The tyres of our vehicles or balloons of our child may depend on air for their existence and functioning, but air itself is not dependent on anything for its existence or functioning. Likewise, all milk products are dependent on milk, all jewellery dependent on gold, not vice versa.

Universes are created and destroyed constantly, but that has no effect on their source, the universal energy or God. The universal energy always exists in its unmanifested form, though we get to see it only when it is manifested.

Day 5

Look at the power of my divine mystery. In reality, I, the sustainer and creator of all beings, am not in them, and they also are not in me. In fact, the gold chain is nothing but gold. Also, matter and energy are different as well as non-different. (9.05)

The universal energy or super-soul exists as soul in all living beings, creating and supporting them, yet not getting entangled in them. This entire activity is done in a detached manner. It is similar to a person dreaming all kinds of dreams, yet not really participating in them.

Each cell of our body is alive because of the universal energy. We can safely say that God is in every cell of all living beings. But do we behave like God? No, we do not. Instead, we live in the delusion created by the material world with the help of our senses, and are subject to a never-ending cycle of birth and death.

Gold and gold ornaments are not the same when you look at them, yet they are the same in essence. Matter or nature and energy or soul are different, yet they are from the same source, the universal energy, hence non-different too.

Day 6

Perceive that all beings remain in me—without any contact or without producing any effect—as the mighty wind, moving everywhere, eternally remains in space. (9.06)

The space is an endless expanse. It contains the earth, moon, sun, other planets and stars. For us, the earthlings, air is an infinitely vast part of nature. It affects all living beings. Lack of air or polluted air can kill, whereas fresh air revives. Air in motion becomes wind, and depending on its speed, it can create havoc, destroying everything coming in its way.

In whatever form it might be at any given point of time, air would always remain contained in space, as are other things. Space is not affected by any actions of air, nor is it affected by the absence or presence of any things or beings. It just serves as an inert container of all beings and other things.

At a micro level, whatever we do with our body does not affect our soul. We have already established the fact that it's the body that grows old and not the soul.

Day 7

All beings merge into my primary material nature at the end of a time-cycle (kalpa), and I create them again at the beginning of the next cycle. (9.07)

God's creation is like a film. It runs on the screen till the time its reel is running in the projector. Once the reel ends, the projection on the screen ends, the film ends. Then it starts all over again, for the next show.

The people who are watching the film get affected by whatever is happening in it; they laugh or cry or clap as they watch the story unfold. The person who is running the reel in the projection room is not affected by the film. He just does his job of running the film many times in a day.

In the same manner, God creates and annihilates the universe. At the end of a time-cycle, the entire creation is annihilated and it merges back into its source, the universal energy or God. After another time-cycle, the process of creation starts again, and so it goes on. These cycles of creation and dissolution are eternal and God remains unaffected all through them.

Day 8

I create the entire multitude of beings again and again with the help of my material nature. These beings are under control of the three modes of nature. (9.08)

There are three modes of material nature that influence the way a person thinks or behaves. Sattvic nature makes a person peaceful, rajasic nature results in passion and tamasic nature makes one lazy. These three modes of nature control the living beings.

The universal energy or God creates living beings with the help of material nature. The beings, while being under the influence of the three modes of nature, get trapped in the sensory temptations of the material world around them. This dictates their actions or karma.

Based on their karma, the living beings are reborn and this cycle of death and rebirth goes on forever.

Day 9

These acts of creation do not bind me because I remain indifferent and unattached to the acts. (9.09)

Though God is responsible for the entire creation, he is unattached to it. Like a judge passing judgment, God creates beings based on the karma of their past life. The entire process is conducted with mathematical precision and no emotion.

God is neither attached to creation nor to annihilation of the universe. It is attachment to the fruit of action that binds. It is the feeling of 'I did this' that creates attachment. Since all of God's actions are done with detachment, there is no question of attachment and bonds.

This is the message hidden in this verse. If we let go of egoism and doership of any work, we would also become detached from the fruit of our actions.

Day 10

The divine kinetic energy (maya), with the help of material nature, creates all animate and inanimate objects under my supervision, and thus the creation keeps on going. (9.10)

The Supreme soul or God, although aloof from the activities of the material world, remains the supreme director. The source of the divine kinetic energy as well as material nature is the Supreme soul.

All the living entities are born under the glance or light of the Supreme soul, but take different bodies according to their past deeds and desires. So, the Supreme soul is not directly attached to the creation, though it activates it.

On the other hand, the material nature gives birth to all living entities and, hence, is also called Mother nature—though in reality the Supreme soul is the unseen source or mother of all.

So we can see that by the presence of the Supreme soul or God, the wheel of manifested and unmanifested beings revolves round and round forever.

Day 11

I am the ritual, I am the sacrifice, I am the offering, I am the herb, I am the mantra, I am the clarified butter, I am the fire and I am the oblation. (9.16)

The Vedic sacrificial ceremonies are called *yagyas* and *yagnas*. They involve praying to fire with offerings of clarified butter and herbs while chanting sacred words or mantras. Clarified butter is made from cow's milk and hence represents the animal kingdom, whereas the herbs represent the plant kingdom.

After the earth was created, along with its landmass and water bodies, the next step was the creation of plants, animals and all forms of living beings. Since all the living beings come from one source, they are the expression of the universal energy in different forms.

The Vedic ritual is interpreted as an offering of nature to the universal energy or the source. What we receive from the source, we surrender back to it. It also indicates that all forms of worship are essentially the same, we worship the universal energy, the one source or God, using his own various forms.

Day 12

I am the supporter of the universe, the father, the mother and the grandfather. I am the object of knowledge, the sacred syllable AUM, and the Rig, Saam and Yajur vedas. (9.17)

The entire universe, moving and non-moving, is manifested through the different activities of the universal energy or God.

In the material world, we have relationships like those of father, mother, grandfather and so on. They are also a part of the same universal energy. God is in every living being.

The knowledge of the universal energy or God is the only knowledge to be had; the rest follows automatically. All our education, the various subjects we study, are of no use if they increase our bonds of attachment to the material world.

The understanding of Self, of the eternal soul, is true knowledge that frees us from the cycle of rebirths. The vedas direct us to this knowledge.

Day 13

I am the goal, the supporter, the Lord, the witness, the abode, the refuge, the friend, the origin, the dissolution, the foundation, the treasure-house and the immutable seed. (9.18)

The universal energy or the super-soul is the source of everything and hence, is also the goal for all to merge into. The infinite mass of energy not only creates but also supports the entire creation in itself. It is also the Lord or controller of all creation. But with all its activity, the universal energy remains an ever detached witness or observer. The entire universe is created from it and is also dissolved into it, and yet does not affect it in the least.

The universal energy is also compared to a seed, though an imperishable one, as it gives rise to all forms of creation. All living beings take birth according to their past deeds and desires, the knowledge of which is stored like a treasure in the source itself. This treasure house has all the information about our past, present and future.

Finally, since God is our creator, our father, there can be no better refuge or friend than him.

Day 14

I give heat, I send as well as withhold the rain. I am immortality as well as death, I am also both the eternal Absolute and the Temporal. (9.19)

Krishna presents himself, or the universal energy, as the great paradox, as the one responsible for the pairs of opposites—heat-cold, life-death, reality-illusion.

The universal energy has created the sun to give us heat and light. The sun is also responsible for climatic changes resulting in cold weather, rains as well as drought.

Since the universal energy is our life-breath, the source of our life, it's withdrawal results in death. So, what gives life gives death as well.

The entire universe is the manifested energy of the Supreme, in various shapes and forms according to their karmic past. But then, creation is a constant process. The ones yet to be born, still unmanifest, are also a part of the universal energy.

Day 15

The doers of the rituals prescribed in the vedas, the devoted, and whose sins are cleansed, worship me by doing good deeds for gaining heaven. As a result of their meritorious deeds they go to heaven and enjoy celestial sense pleasures. (9.20)

The vedas prescribe a number of rituals to appease the various gods for gaining wealth, gaining scriptural knowledge, getting a good harvest, fighting terminal disease, getting a good spouse and so on. All these gods are also a part of the universal energy, though not the energy itself.

Apart from specific rituals, there are generic rituals for atoning our sins and clearing the path towards heaven. Going to heaven after death is probably the most favourite death wish of people.

As mentioned earlier, heaven, hell and earth are three realms of the universe. In heaven, there might be celestial pleasures to enjoy, but only for a limited period of time. After that, the soul returns to earth to fulfil the leftover desires from its past. The cycle of rebirth doesn't end.

Day 16

They return to the mortal world after enjoying the wide world of heavenly pleasures, upon exhaustion of the fruits of their good karma. Thus, following the injunctions of the vedas, persons working for the fruit of their actions take repeated births. (9.21)

According to the Vedic theory, those who perform the rituals gain heavenly enjoyments after death. But going to heaven is not the ultimate goal of the soul; it's goal is to merge with its source, the super-soul or the universal energy.

Wanting to go to heaven is also a sensory desire, and like other such desires, it is also time-bound. The time period depends on the quantum of good karma that the soul has accomplished in its lifetime. This period, whether long or short, eventually ends and the soul resumes its never-ending journey of rebirths.

According to Krishna, humans operate from the ego-centric consciousness. They always seek pleasure, either of this world or of heaven, and therefore, are stuck in the ever-running Ferris wheel of life and death.

Day 17

I personally take care of both spiritual and material welfare of those ever-steadfast devotees who always remember and adore me with single-minded contemplation. (9.22)

This is the core of Krishna's discourse. It states that God takes care of all the burdens of his devotees. Devotion here means unconditional love for God, abandoning all other love and attachments, and faith that God would look after us and protect us like a father does for his child.

After gaining control of our senses and dropping all attachments to the material world, devoting ourselves to selfless service, the next step is unswerving devotion to God. This state of mind at the time of death results in the soul's merging with the super-soul or God.

Most people foolishly spend their lives in the pursuit of material wealth, which they have to leave behind when they die. But the wise spend their time to find wisdom, which frees them from the cycle of rebirth.

Day 18

Even those devotees who worship the deities with faith, they also worship me, but in an improper way. (9.23)

Not everyone in the world prays to the same God. People pray to deities of their choice, some pray to saints, prophets or incarnations, others to symbols that give them comfort. All of these, in reality, are various aspects of universal energy or God.

So, when people are worshipping different deities with full faith, they are actually invoking the same energy expressed through different forms.

Hence, Krishna says that even though people may worship other deities, they are indirectly worshipping him. The destination is the same, even though the routing is different.

Day 19

I, the Supreme Being, alone am the enjoyer of all sacrificial services, and Lord of the universe. But people do not know my true transcendental nature. Therefore, they fall into the repeated cycles of birth and death. (9.24)

When a person watering plants sprays water only on the leaves and branches, they think they have done their job. The plants look clean too. Actually, the roots have to be watered for the proper growth of the plants. When the roots are healthy, the entire plant remains healthy. Watering just the leaves and branches may eventually result in the water trickling down to the roots, but it would not be enough to sustain the entire plant.

According to Krishna, the people who pray to various deities are ignorant. They do not pray to the infinite God, but to his finite manifestations.

A devotee can rise only up to the object and objective of his worship. Hence, the finite gods take him to a finite level, that of heaven, from where he has to eventually return to the mortal world. Such a devotee continues to be born into the mundane mortal world again and again.

Day 20

Worshippers of the celestial controllers go to the celestial controllers, the worshippers of the ancestors go to the ancestors, and the worshippers of the ghosts go to the ghosts, but my devotees come to me, and are not born again. (9.25)

The celestial controllers represent the various sense organs, through which the material world is experienced. It is a realm of physical experiences. Those who consistently desire the external world of joys and successes and pray to the appropriate deities manage to gain such enjoyments.

The ancestors represent cultural purity and traditions. The worshippers of ancestors gain the beauty and perfection of a pure life. The ghosts represent nature and nature worshippers attain success depending on their efforts.

But these are limited forms of the Supreme energy and cannot give the ultimate peace and bliss that is achieved by worshipping the source. Devotion to the Supreme brings the reward of merging with the source, never to enter the cycle of rebirth.

Day 21

Whosoever offers me a leaf, a flower, a fruit, or water with devotion, I accept that offering. (9.26)

A gift is an offering of love or affection or devotion. The emotions associated with the gift make it precious. If the emotions are not genuine, however expensive the gift might be, its value is nothing to the receiver.

Krishna's life was his teaching. There are many instances in his life where he accepts the humble gifts of devotees and rewards them with phenomenal riches. One such famous incident was that of Sudama, a childhood friend of Krishna. Sudama was a great devotee of Krishna and when he falls into dire times, he decides to seek Krishna's help.

Sudama had nothing except a fistful of rice flakes to offer as a gift to Krishna. True to what he preached, Krishna accepted that humble gift with great love and showered unmeasurable riches on Sudama and his family, changing their lives forever. According to Krishna, surrender of Self is the biggest gift ever.

Day 22

Whatever you do, whatever you eat, whatever you offer as oblation to the sacred fire, whatever charity you give, whatever austerity you perform, do all that as an offering unto me. (9.27)

Since the universal energy is the source of everything in the universe, it is obvious that what we eat or offer to the sacred fire as oblation, is also a part of universal energy. Why do we make the offering? The idea behind doing that is to show our devotion to the universal energy or God.

An offering is a token of our love, that is why a lot of people like giving to charities. The charities help and support the needy and underprivileged, so helping a charity is helping them. Again, the needy are also living beings, coming from the same source as us.

Since all our offerings are going to the various manifestations of the Supreme, it is suggested that we actively, consciously think of the Supreme while doing anything—be it our personal work or charity. This would ensure a constant remembrance of God, helping us to make it our final destination post death.

Day 23

You shall become free from the bondage of actions yielding good or bad karma and come to me by this attitude of complete renunciation. (9.28)

The dictionary meaning of renunciation is the formal rejection of something, typically a belief, claim or course of action. People misconstrue it to mean physically leaving the material world, family, wealth, etc., and living in the wilderness, or better still, the snowy Himalayas. This is absolutely contrary to what Krishna has advocated.

Krishna advises to renounce the fruits of action. He advises to reject egocentric activities and cravings. Rejection of the physical world is simpler, but running away from temptations does not guarantee that our cravings have ended. People who fast or are on a particular diet are constantly thinking of the food that they are not supposed to eat.

When we renounce the fruits of our action, we are able to focus more on the action. It's the attachment to the fruits, the desire for favourable results, that binds us to any action. Detachment gives us freedom from karmic bondage. It makes us act selflessly for the larger good of the people of the society, or even the country.

An unattached soul has no reason to return to the mortal world; it merges with its source.

Day 24

The Self is present equally in all beings. There is no one hateful or dear to me. But, those who worship me with love and devotion are very close to me, and I am also very close to them. (9.29)

The sun shines on everything in the world; its rays get reflected from all kinds of surfaces, whether smooth or rough. Likewise, the universal energy is present in everything in the universe and illumines the thoughts and emotions of all living beings.

The quality of reflection of the sun's rays may vary due to the variation in the reflective surface. But that doesn't mean the sun is shining more or less on those surfaces. In the same way, some people show better spiritual advancement than others. It does not mean that the Self or God is partial towards them.

But then, the closer we are to the Self, the closer it is to us. It simply means that the more understanding we have of the universal energy, the higher the chances are of our merging with it. A simple analogy would be of fire. The closer you are to it, the warmer you get; the further you are, the colder you are.

Day 25

Even if the most sinful person resolves to worship me with single-minded loving devotion, such a person must be regarded as a saint because of making the right resolution. (9.30)

Better late than never, they say. Prophets and preachers of all religious faiths have been expounding this fact. The main thing is to realize where we have gone wrong. Acceptance is the first step to resolving the problem. Hence, if the worst of sinners realizes his mistakes and decides to follow the path of light, he should be respected.

It is not easy even for a normal person, who is not sinning but is lost in the sensory material world, to understand the difference between the mortal body and the immortal soul. So, if someone has realized the cosmic truth, his being a sinner in the past is irrelevant.

Repentance is a genuine change of heart. It includes regret for the past actions and a decision to prevent a repetition in the future. We know that it's very difficult to control our senses. But if we surrender to the universal energy or God, the task becomes simpler, and we are able to drop our attachments, even to our past. Such a detached person is considered to be saintly.

Day 26

Such a person soon becomes righteous and attains everlasting peace. Be aware that my devotee shall never perish or fall down. (9.31)

A person who realizes that they have sinned in the past has obviously awakened their sense of discrimination. This is an important step forward. Once this is in place, the person can pause and review their life where they would be able to see where they had committed mistakes and what were those mistakes. Since they cannot wind the clock back, they resolve to not repeat their mistakes. This is the next important step.

Even with all the resolutions in place, it's not easy for the person to control their senses at all times. They need to distract themself and shift their attention elsewhere, and that 'elsewhere' is the universal energy or God. This step takes them on to the path of light.

Absolute focus on the universal energy helps the person realize the energy in themselves, in their soul. Such a person is now free of all worldly agitations and attains everlasting peace.

10

Manifestation of the Absolute

27 July–3 August

Day 27

Neither the celestial controllers, nor the great sages know my origin because I am the origin of celestial controllers and great sages also. (10.02)

The universal energy is changeless and immutable, yet it manifests its glories in the universe through various forms. Though it is unborn and eternal, it is the cause of all that is born and perishable. The mystery of these manifestations is not known even to the celestial controllers, the gods of the senses and the great sages.

The origin of the universal energy is unknown, as it's the most ancient and was present before anything and everything else. The demi-gods and sages cannot have any knowledge about the origin of the universal energy, as they themselves originated from it.

This universal energy or God reveals himself in the hearts of his devotees.

Day 28

One who knows me as the unborn, the beginning-less, and the Supreme Lord of the universe, is considered wise among the mortals and becomes liberated from the bondage of karma. (10.03)

Knowing a person or a thing would normally mean having a reasonable knowledge about them. But here, the meaning is a bit different. According to Krishna, knowing him or the universal energy is more spiritual and emotional. One has to experience the energy, the Self within, to 'know' it.

Since the universal energy is eternal and infinite and is never expressed in any finite form, it is considered unborn or birthless. Waves are born in the ocean and they dissolve in the ocean too, while the ocean remains birthless. Every manifestation in the universe has a beginning and an end, it is created in Self and is dissolved in Self, while the Self remains beginning-less and endless.

This knowledge of the universal soul or Self comes from within us when we realize the Self within our own heart. According to Krishna, Self-knowledge liberates us from all karmic bondage.

Day 29

Discrimination, Self-knowledge, forgiveness, truthfulness, control over the mind and senses, tranquillity, fearlessness, non-violence, equanimity, contentment, austerity, charity, fame, ill fame—these diverse qualities in human beings arise from me alone. (10.04–10.05)

The diverse qualities of human beings, whether good or bad, also have their origin in the universal energy.

Discrimination or intelligence is the power to analyse things in their proper perspective, and knowledge means knowing the distinction between Spirit and matter. Freedom from doubt and delusion is achieved when one is detached from sensory temptations. Tolerance and forgiveness are important to move on from attachments.

Truthfulness is required to present the facts for the benefit of others. Control of senses means that senses should not be used for unnecessary personal enjoyment. Likewise, the mind should be restrained from thinking unnecessary thoughts. Non-violence means not doing anything that causes misery to others. Equanimity refers to freedom from attachment and aversion.

All these qualities and more are manifested in human beings as well as demigods in the other realms.

Day 30

The seven great sages and the Manus are modifications of my nature and were born of my thought, with powers like mine. All the living creatures on earth descend from them. (10.06)

This is a genealogical synopsis of the universal population. Brahma was the first manifestation of the universal energy and from him manifested the seven great sages and four Manus.

The vedas were revealed to these seven sages and hence they became the original teachers of the world. The four Manus were the original rulers of the world.

Since the sages and Manus were born of the mind of the Lord and were connected to the universal energy, they also imbibed it within themselves and obtained wisdom and power.

The present inhabitants of the world have descended from these primeval, though illustrious, people.

Day 31

Everything emanates from me. The wise ones who understand this adore me with love and devotion. (10.08)

In the previous verses, we established the fact that the universal energy is the source of everything in the material and spiritual worlds. It is the creator, controller and destroyer of all. It is also the unifying essence running through all experiences and all expressions of life and matter.

'Experiment and theory alike indicate that the universe began in a state of perfect simplicity, evidence of which was burned into the heart of every atom at the beginning of time,' wrote Timothy

Ferris, a science columnist for the New York Times.[3]

The wise ones understand this cosmic truth and are devoted to the creator, the universal energy or God. They are so steadfast in their devotion that they can never be shaken by any other theory or doctrine.

AUGUST

Day 1

I dwell within their inner psyche as consciousness and destroy the darkness born of ignorance by shining the lamp of transcendental knowledge, as an act of compassion for them. (10.11)

The Self is within us, but because we have no knowledge of it, we do not see it. This is implied by the darkness of ignorance.

Krishna explains how devotion to God or the universal energy leads to destruction of ignorance and rise of understanding. This understanding is the light that dispels darkness and reveals the universal energy present in us.

When we ask the right questions and follow the right actions, our inner lamp of wisdom lights up and we snap out of the delusions of the material world. And like everything else, this also happens by the grace of God or the universal energy that is within us and around us.

Day 2

I am the Supreme Spirit (or super-soul) abiding in the inner psyche of all beings. I am also the creator, maintainer and destroyer, or the beginning, the middle and the end of all beings. (10.20)

---

[3]Timothy Ferris, *The Whole Shebang: A State of the University Report*, Simon Schuster, 1998.

This verse is the sum and substance of the entire Gita. Krishna or the universal energy is the origin of the cosmos with all its universes and beings. The material creation happened when the two aspects of the universal energy united. Purush, the Spirit or soul, united with prakriti, the nature, and thus all beings were created.

Once the universes were created, the universal energy or Krishna is manifested as super-soul in each and every entity. The super-soul is present as a witness in us, watching the drama of the soul getting deluded by the sense organs of the physical body. The drama goes on till the body dies and the soul gets reborn in another body and continues to fulfil the leftover desires from the previous life.

Finally, everything dies—the universe is annihilated and gets dissolved back into its source, the universal energy or Krishna.

Hence, Krishna is the beginning of the universe, the maintainer of the universal manifestations, and the end of all energy.

Day 3

I am the all-devouring death, and also the origin of future beings. I am the seven goddesses or guardian angels presiding over the seven qualities of fame, prosperity, speech, memory, intellect, resolve and forgiveness. (10.34)

The moment we are born, we start dying from that very moment. Death is devouring every living entity at every moment and the last or final stroke is called death itself. But as we know, only the body dies, the soul is immortal. The soul takes birth in another body. In a way, the death of one causes birth of another.

It's the universal energy or Krishna who is the cause of and present in every living entity, he is the birth and death of all.

Krishna also presides over the seven qualities or attributes of nature, which may be consciously tapped through deep meditation. These are fame or glory; success or prosperity; speech, an instrument to spread knowledge; memory, to draw upon the vast storehouse of ancient knowledge; intellect, the power to discriminate and maintain harmony; resolve or steadfastness; and forgiveness, the harbinger of peace.

11

Vision of the Cosmic Form of Krishna

4–10 August

Day 4

Behold my hundreds and thousands of multifarious divine forms of different colours and shapes. Behold all the celestial beings, the entire creation, animate-inanimate, and whatever else you like to see, all at one place in my body. (11.05–11.07)

Arjun wanted to see the universal form of Krishna and requested him to show it to him. This, the transcendental form of Krishna, was not the usual manifest form like his hundreds and thousands of other forms. Nobody had ever seen it but Krishna, being Arjun's best friend and mentor, agreed to manifest his universal form briefly.

To see gold in different types of ornaments is easy, because it involves physical perception. But to see different types of ornaments in a block of gold is not easy. It would require vision of the intellect, along with some imagination.

Krishna enabled Arjun to have the insight to see him in his universal form. And in that form were hundreds and thousands of creatures of different colours and shapes. There were living beings and non-living objects, suns, moons and other celestial bodies of varying sizes, and many more seen-unseen objects. It was a fascinating sight indeed.

Day 5

But, you cannot see me with your physical eyes; therefore, I will give you the divine eyes to see my majestic power and glory. (11.08)

The eyes of a man's physical body are adapted to see the world of duality—day and night, birth and death and so on. To see the universal form of Krishna, Arjun needed a different kind of vision, a spiritual vision.

Krishna blessed Arjun with divine vision, which enabled him to see beyond the physical body.

We can acquire certain types of knowledge by our own efforts, knowledge based on the perception of the senses and intellectual activity. But then, there are other types of knowledge too, those related to the spiritual world. This knowledge can only be obtained with God's help.

Day 6

I am death, the mighty destroyer of the world. I have come here to destroy all these people. Even without your participation in the war, all the warriors standing arrayed in the opposing armies shall cease to exist. (11.32)

Among the varied things and beings Arjun saw in the universal form of Krishna, there was one that was particularly horrifying. It was that of an all-devouring giant. On asking about it, Krishna said that it was him as Time or Death, the mighty destroyer of the world.

The destruction of people is decided by the acts committed by them long ago. So, even if Arjun did not want to fight, the war on the battlefield of Kurukshetra would happen. And in that war, all the Kauravas were to die as were most of the Pandavas. Death could not be checked even if Arjun did not fight; they would die in another way.

According to Krishna, it was better for Arjun to perform his duty as a warrior and fight. The people he would kill were destined to die any which way.

Day 7

Therefore, you should get up and attain glory. Conquer your enemies, and enjoy a prosperous kingdom. I have already destroyed all these warriors. You are only an instrument. (11.33)

Everything in this universe is according to the cosmic plan. Our job is to continue performing our duty without wasting time worrying about the results. Renouncing the fruits of action is the key.

We all carry our individual baggage from our past life and spend this life in completing the leftover incomplete tasks, fulfilling the leftover desires. As our past decided our present, our present decides our future. The entire universe runs on this formula. Each soul functions independently, though they may live together. As can be seen, we all are just instruments for the execution of God's cosmic plan.

This is what Krishna told Arjun in the battlefield. The warriors were destined to die, Arjun was only an instrument and not the cause of their death. The cause of their death was their own karmic baggage from the past.

Day 8

Pleased with you I have shown you, through my own yogic powers, this particular supreme, shining, universal, infinite and primal form of mine that has never been seen before by anyone other than you. (11.47)

Having heard so much about Krishna as the universal energy creating, maintaining and destroying the universe, Arjun had become curious, like any other human being. He wanted to see the universal form of Krishna.

Krishna obliged his dear friend, also his favourite devotee, and manifested his effulgent universal form using his yogic powers. This was a rare feat and Krishna did it because he loved Arjun.

No one in the universe had witnessed this infinite form of Krishna, the universal energy. How could they? After all, it was an unmanifest form, a form that contained the entire universe.

Because of Arjun, Krishna manifested his primal form, which was also seen by other devotees in the various other realms of the universe. This was also a way to validate what Krishna had been saying all this while.

Day 9

However, through single-minded devotion alone, I can be seen in this form, can be known in essence, and also can be reached. (11.54)

Devotion is the sole means to realizing the Supreme. In unconditional, unswerving devotion, which seeks none other than the Supreme, nothing else than the Supreme is experienced by the sense organs. Before devotion sets in, the sense organs are reeling under the onslaught of worldly temptations. Devotion also serves as a cleanser of senses.

Neither philosophical speculation nor studying of the scriptures can explain the phenomenon of Krishna. The vedas prescribe various rituals to understand Krishna, but any theoretical learning is not as effective as practical experience.

When mention is made, about seeing the form, it is actually not the physical seeing, but experiencing it. The Self or Krishna is experienced within. The essence is felt. This is known as 'reaching' him.

Day 10

The one who does all works for me, and to whom I am the supreme goal, who is my devotee, who has no attachment and is free from enmity towards any being, attains me. (11.55)

This is the substance of the entire teaching of the Gita. According to it, the art of right living comprises five major ingredients. The first is to dedicate all our work to God, without seeking any rewards for ourselves.

The second is to make reaching God or Self-realization our goal in life. Serving God with our heart and soul, through serving people, is the third ingredient. This requires seeing every living being as an image of God.

Detachment from the material world is a very crucial fourth ingredient, which leads to the fifth and last ingredient—feeling no hatred or enmity towards anyone in the world. One who possesses these five ingredients is sure to attain God.

12

Path of Bhakti Yoga

11–25 August

Day 11

Those ever steadfast devotees who worship with supreme faith by fixing their mind on my personal form of God, I consider them to be the best yogis. (12.02)

This is for people who worship idols. Three conditions should be fulfilled to get the best results. The first condition is that the idol should be of Krishna. And when worshipping it, the mind should think of his universal form. Thought is the source of activity in the mind and intellect. Hence it is important for it to go into the vastness of the universe created by Krishna.

The second condition is that of steadfastness of mind. We know how mercurial the mind is, and how it has the tendency to get distracted midway during any activity. To worship Krishna, self-control is needed to keep the mind focussed on the object of worship. This comes when one is detached from the material world.

The final condition is to have supreme faith. This is not blind belief in what anyone might be saying. Supreme faith comes from understanding that God is in everything and everything is in God. Those fulfilling these conditions are considered to be sincere yogis.

Day 12

But those who worship the unchangeable, the inexplicable, the invisible, the omnipresent and the formless impersonal aspect of God; restraining all the senses, even-minded under all circumstances, engaged in the welfare of all creatures, also attain God. (12.03–12.04)

This is for those who worship the unmanifest, abstract form of God. The unmanifest universal energy is invisible, and since it can't be perceived, it is inconceivable and inexplicable or indefinable. The energy is formless and omnipresent, hence immovable; since it is present everywhere, there is no place left for it to move into. The universal energy supports the creation, maintenance and destruction of universes, yet remains unchangeable, imperishable and eternal.

The seeker who worships the unmanifest should follow three conditions. He should have mastery over his senses, so that he is able to focus on the unmanifest. Intellectual equanimity, in all conditions and situations while living in the material world, is a fundamental requirement for successful meditation on the unmanifest. Lastly, the seeker should be ever ready to help others to the best of his ability.

Fulfilling these conditions would help the seeker reach God, as the goal is the same.

Day 13

Self-realization is more difficult for those who fix their mind on the impersonal, unmanifest and formless Absolute because comprehension of the unmanifest by embodied beings is attained with difficulty. (12.05)

According to Krishna, because it's the abstract idea of God or universal energy, it is not always easy to focus on the unmanifest, especially for the embodied beings. Embodied here stands for those who identify with their bodies, like you and me.

For most of us, it is easy to understand physical forms, as that is how we exist and that is how we see things around us. This is the reason why idol worship is popular. There is an instant connect and instant focus on the object of worship. And to simplify things further, we have created the idol of God in our own image—as a perfect human being.

Worshipping the unmanifest is challenging as there is nothing to focus on, in the infinite. The mortal brains are tuned to look for forms. When we look up at the sky during the day, our attention is grabbed by the clouds; in the night it is the stars. But even then, though comprehension of the formless is not easy, it is doable by those who have decided to do it.

Day 14

For those who worship me with unswerving devotion as a personal deity of their choice, offering all actions to me, intent on me as the Supreme, and meditate on me; I swiftly become their saviour from the mortal world. (12.06-07)

Krishna lays down certain instructions to be followed by those who want to worship the manifest form of God. The first is to renounce the fruit of all actions and offer the actions to Krishna. This entails complete surrender to God, renouncing our ego.

The second is to make Krishna our personal deity and direct our energies to achieve the goal of self-perfection in the image of God. This is something like what the youngsters do—they put up posters of their hero or heroine in their room and aim to become like him or her. This is the genesis of the term 'idolizing'.

The last instruction is to take our mind away from distracting thoughts and focus single-pointedly on Krishna, with the dominant thought of merging our soul with the super-soul. To such a devotee, Krishna becomes the saviour, freeing them from the cycle of rebirths in this mortal world.

Day 15

Therefore, focus your mind on me, and let your intellect dwell upon me alone through meditation and contemplation. Thereafter you shall certainly attain me. (12.08)

Krishna tells Arjun how to disconnect his mind and discrimination from the senses and direct them to inner perception in order to experience the soul consciousness. This instruction is relevant for all of us.

By meditation, focussing the mind on the form of Krishna is possible. The important thing here would be to give up all thoughts of sense objects. The mind may seem simple enough to focus, the problem arises from our intellect.

Our intellect has the habit of weighing things, discriminating right from wrong, determining what action to take, and so on. So, the intellect also has to focus on Krishna.

Finally, when the intellect understands the infinite universal energy and the mind focuses on the manifest form of that energy as Krishna, Self-realization is attained.

Day 16

If you are unable to focus your mind steadily on me, then seek to attain me by practice of any other spiritual discipline; such as a ritual or deity worship that suits you. (12.09)

In case one is unable to focus their mind steadily on him, Krishna has another option for them.

The first step to focus our mind on anything is to calm the mind. Normal human minds are very restless. We have so much to think about. There always seem to be job interviews, exams, targets to achieve at work, household problems, issues of children and other family members, health issues, financial issues and many such seemingly mundane problems in our lives.

Yoga helps to focus on one's breath in relation to one's body. Some people prefer regular chanting at fixed times of the day. Some like to visit holy shrines, while some fast on certain days of the week or month.

According to Krishna, any spiritual discipline that helps us in stilling our mind is good. Only when our mind is still can we focus on Krishna.

Day 17

If you are unable to do any spiritual discipline, then be intent on performing your duty just for me. You shall attain perfection by doing your prescribed duty for me, without any selfish motive, but just as an instrument to serve and please me. (12.10)

Some people, in fact most people, are too distracted to follow any spiritual discipline in their lives. They don't have any time for it, they say. Every minute of their busy day is accounted for. Well, Krishna has an option for them too.

There is no need to take out time from one's busy schedule for any spiritual activity. Only one thing needs to be done—remembering God while doing any work. It's not difficult to do so; it's just a question of getting into the habit of remembering someone.

When we lose a loved one, we tend to remember them at all times or at least most of the time; when we are in love, we think of our lover all the time, don't we? In the same way, we can think of God while we are performing any task. Instead of pleasing ourselves or anyone else, we can direct our action to please God. It may seem difficult initially, but would soon become a habit. Without realizing it, we would shift the focus of our mind to God or Krishna.

Day 18

If you are unable to do your duty for me, then just surrender unto my will, and renounce the attachment to and the anxiety for the fruits of all work by learning to accept all results as God's grace with equanimity. (12.11)

It may be that due to family or religious constraints, one is unable to dedicate all of one's actions to Krishna. There is yet another option for them.

One needs to just cultivate a simple faith in God, in any form, and try to unselfishly perform actions without focussing on their results. By doing this, one's mind would become free of likes and dislikes that are normally part of selfish activities.

When a restless person meditates without any preconditioned expectation of results, they meditate better. Why? Because their mind is not distracted by cravings for any result.

Once this aspect of working is sorted out, the next is to accept all results of the work as God's grace.

Day 19

The transcendental knowledge of scriptures is better than mere ritualistic practice; meditation is better than scriptural knowledge; renunciation of selfish attachment to the fruits of work (karma yoga) is better than meditation; peace immediately follows renunciation of selfish motives. (12.12)

Listening to discourses on scriptures is normally considered as a spiritual practice, as is performing rituals without understanding the significance behind them. According to Krishna, knowledge is better than mere practice. Knowledge means acquiring discrimination power and discipline at mental and intellectual levels. A correct knowledge of any spiritual practice is essential for it to be fruitful.

Better than just acquiring knowledge, is meditating over it, which means pondering over its deeper meaning. But meditation may not be successful if the mind is agitated due to all kinds of anxieties.

Therefore, renunciation of the fruits of action is recommended. It is even better than meditation. It teaches self-control and relieves the mind of all its agitations. Once the mind is rid of all its desires, peace follows.

Day 20

One who does not hate any creature, is compassionate, is free from the notion of 'I' and 'mine', is even-minded in pain and pleasure, is ever content, who has subdued the mind, whose resolve is firm, whose mind and intellect are engaged in dwelling upon me, who is devoted to me—is dear to me. (12.13–12.14)

The person who perceives the same Spirit in all creation cannot feel hatred for any creature, and would be naturally friendly and compassionate to all. Such a person would not see anyone as an enemy. The person who has subdued the ego, does not think in terms of 'I' and 'mine'.

The person who has full control over his senses remains ever content under all conditions of existence. Such a person also remains unruffled by material sufferings and pleasures.

Steadfast in his belief in Krishna as the Supreme God, such a devotee is dear to him and soon achieves his goal of Self-realization.

Day 21

The one by whom others are not agitated and who is not agitated by others, who is free from joy, envy, fear and anxiety, is also dear to me. (12.15)

There are some people like Mother Teresa or Mahatma Gandhi,

whose personas are very calming. Their mere presence changes the environment of any place.

In an emergency room of any hospital, the doctors are trained to remain calm under all circumstances because, if they get agitated, they would make mistakes and a doctor's mistake invariably turns out to be fatal. A mind blinded by agitation is unable to discriminate between right and wrong.

How does one get rid of agitations? By controlling the senses. It is the senses that create desires and the related emotions of joy, envy, fear or anxiety. Our friend owns a beautiful solitaire ring, which causes us envy. We save up and manage to buy a bigger solitaire for ourselves. But the joy is short-lived as we fear for its safety. The story can go on forever. These kind of emotions agitate the mind.

When the mind is desireless, it is free from agitations. Such a saintly person is a Self-realized soul.

Day 22

One who is desireless, pure, wise, impartial and free from anxiety, who has renounced the doership in all undertakings, such a devotee is dear to me. (12.16)

Self-realized people are free from worldly expectations and, hence, free from all anxieties. Their happiness does not depend on the well-being of their physical body or sense pleasures or acquisition of material wealth. Having realized the Self, such people are in a state of permanent bliss. Their actions are ever selfless and devoted to help others, as they see the same Self in all living beings. They know that in serving others they are serving God.

Even if such people are running a big business, they run it not for their personal gratification, but for the larger good of society. A classic example would be of Bill and Melinda Gates, who decided to use 95 per cent of their wealth for charitable activities across the globe.[4] Mark Zuckerberg has also pledged 50 per cent of his wealth for charity work as have Warren Buffett,[5] Azim Premji and Nandan Nilekani.

There are many such people in the world who think more about others than themselves. They can be termed as modern day saints.

Day 23

One who neither rejoices nor grieves, neither likes nor dislikes, who has renounced both the good and the evil, and is full of devotion, is dear to me. (12.17)

According to Krishna, a true yogi is devout in all aspects of life. Their mental equilibrium is not affected by good fortune or calamity. They are not overpowered by grief under any circumstances, are free from material longings. They have essentially risen above the duality of good and evil.

When a devotee has awakened to God-consciousness, has realized Self, they start looking at the world differently. Such a person sees God in everyone, as they have realized that the universal energy pervades the entire creation.

Since now they are the controller of their own senses, the duality of the material world does not bother them anymore. They neither rejoice nor grieve, neither like nor dislike; in fact, their sole focus in life is to serve God in every way possible.

---

[4]"Bill and Melinda Gates give 95% of wealth to charity", BBC News, 18 October 2010, https://www.bbc.com/news/av/entertainment-arts-11565953.
[5]Dominic Rushe, 'Facebook founder Mark Zuckerberg signs up for Giving Pledge', *The Guardian*, 9 December 2010, https://www.theguardian.com/technology/2010/dec/09/mark-zuckerberg-signs-up-for-giving-pledge.

Day 24

The one who remains the same towards a friend or foe, in honour or disgrace, in heat or cold, in pleasure or pain; who is free from attachment; who is indifferent to censure or praise; who is quiet and content with whatever he has; unattached to a place, a country, or a house; equanimous and full of devotion; that person is dear to me. (12.18–12.19)

The wise understand the world to be a dream of God, like a film. Friends and foes, honour or disgrace, the experiences of heat and cold, pleasure and pain in their daily life are a source of entertainment to them. They know them to be as meaningless, ever-changing shadows of delusion.

They don't speak much, speaking only what is required and when it's required. They are content with whatever they have and whatever they get, as they have very few needs.

The wise are unattached to a place, country or house, as they are devoid of any feeling of possession or belonging. Such souls are meant to serve humanity as a whole and cannot be bound to any place.

Day 25

Those faithful devotees, who set me as their supreme goal and follow, or just sincerely try to develop the above mentioned nectar of moral values, are very dear to me. (12.20)

Krishna encourages people to set him as their main goal in life because what one sets as a goal, one achieves.

He wants them to understand the cosmic reality. He wants them to know that the perishable physical body and the imperishable soul have been manifested by one universal energy, that is him. He is the creator, maintainer and destroyer of the entire creation.

He wants people to learn to keep their senses in control, so that they are not caught in the web of sensory desires. The material world is full of temptations that keep the soul engaged in the cycle of rebirths.

Krishna tells people that the only way to break away from the karmic cycle is to follow him, develop the moral values suggested by him and work selflessly to serve him. Doing that, they would focus their energies on him, and eventually realize him within themselves. This should be the goal of every soul—to merge with the source.

13

Creation and the Creator

26 August–16 September

Day 26

This physical body, the miniature universe, may be called the field or creation. One who knows the creation is called the knower (or soul) by the seers of truth. (13.01)

Our body is the field of activity for the soul. This is where the seeds of karma, good or bad, are sown and reaped after appropriate time. This is where events happen, including growth, decline and death.

The individual soul is the knower of the field. The soul is entrapped and conditioned by the material existence and wants to lord it over the latter. And to do that it gets a field of activity, which is the body.

The third entity is the conscious Self, the observer, the super-soul. He is the Supreme Lord, the universal energy or Krishna—the source and controller of everything.

The body, the miniature universe, is also termed prakriti or nature. It is an unconscious activity. The individual soul is also termed purush or matter. It is inactive consciousness. The super-soul, also termed Ishwara, is inactive and detached.

Day 27

Know me to be the creator of all the creation. The true understanding of both the creator and the creation is considered by me to be the transcendental knowledge. (13.02)

In every living body, there are two souls: the individual soul and the super-soul. The individual soul is the knower of its own body, but the super-soul is the knower of all the bodies of all the species of life.

A farmer may be the knower of his piece of land, but the king would be the knower of all the land, including the farmer's. Likewise, the super-soul is the controller of the soul as well as the body, whereas the individual soul only controls the body.

To understand the soul and super-soul to be one, yet distinct, is transcendental knowledge, according to Krishna.

Krishna, being the super-soul, is the knower and controller of all creation.

Day 28

Humility, modesty, non-violence, forgiveness, honesty, service to guru, purity, steadfastness, self-control, detachment from sense objects, absence of ego, perception of pain and suffering inherent in birth, old age, disease and death—describe the knower of the field. (13.08–13.09)

We can realize the super-soul in us only by overpowering the enslaving power that the material world has on our bodily field. This is done by refusing to get dissolved in the material world, which means resistance and suffering. Accepting the material world and its conventions diminishes suffering and refusal increases it. But then, suffering is the only process through which we fight for our true nature.

Krishna has described elements of knowledge and practices conducive to spiritual enlightenment. Humility, modesty, non-violence, forgiveness, honesty and service to guru are simple enough to understand. Purity here is of body as well as mind. Steadfastness in achieving the spiritual goal and self-control in terms of dealing with others are important elements for this task.

Detachment and absence of ego are prerequisites for spiritual development. Reflection on the miseries of birth, old age, disease and death leads to indifference to sense pleasures. And the senses turn inwards towards the innermost Self or super-soul for knowledge. This was the turning point in Prince Siddhartha's life too, which eventually led him to become the Buddha.

Day 29

Non-attachment, non-fondness of son, wife and home; equanimity in desirable and undesirable circumstances; unswerving devotion to me through single-minded contemplation; taste for solitude, distaste for social gatherings and gossip; steadfastness in acquiring the knowledge of Spirit and seeing the omnipresent Supreme Being everywhere, this is said to be knowledge. That which is contrary to this is ignorance. (13.10–13.12)

When a person thinks that a thing belongs to them, they begin to identify with it, love it and get attached to it. Non-attachment is the absence of any such identification with anything. The same applies to people too. Equanimity is a side-effect of non-attachment. Such a mind seeks solitude and lives within itself; it doesn't like the crowd of other thoughts. Hence, seekers stay away from social gatherings and gossip.

The knowledge of Self is not like any other subject; it has to be lived and not merely learnt. Since Self is everywhere, consistency of living the spiritual knowledge is very important for the seeker. Knowledge includes practice of moral virtues and keeping the goal of Self in front of us at all times. It is this knowledge which is the means for the soul to get out of the material entrapment.

Anything contrary to all this is ignorance. Qualities like pride, hypocrisy, cruelty, impatience, insincerity, etc., tend to empower and perpetuate the material world further and hence should be avoided.

Day 30

The super-soul has its hands, feet, eyes, heads, mouths and ears everywhere because it is all-pervading and omnipresent. (13.13)

As the sun shines, diffusing its unlimited rays of light everywhere, so does the super-soul. It pervades the entire creation from Brahma to the tiniest of insects. Hence, it has unlimited hands, feet, heads, eyes, ears and mouths. This statement is symbolic and shows the omnipresence of the super-soul because actually it is not a being, but a subtle, invisible consciousness or energy.

Nothing can be termed as living if it doesn't have consciousness. Consciousness is life. The functioning of all the parts of our body are based on consciousness or life principle. The functions of perception, feeling and thinking are carried out as long as there is life in the body. This consciousness, which is in every living being, is also called Paramatma or superior to the individual soul, the atma.

Krishna had mentioned earlier that he accepted the smallest of gifts, if given with sincere love, from his devotees. The fact that there must be millions of devotees scattered in the world, offering their gifts at all times, how does he accept them all? Well, the answer is simple—he, being the super-soul, is present everywhere at all times and available to accept our gifts.

Day 31

He is the perceiver of all sense objects without the physical sense organs; unattached and yet the supporter of all; devoid of the three modes of material nature, and yet the enjoyer of the modes of nature by becoming a living entity. (13.14)

The Self or consciousness in us is functioning through the sense organs, providing each of them its own individual faculty. It seems as though it possesses them. But the sense organs decay and perish, while the consciousness is changeless and eternal. It is like electricity, which is not the light that we see in the bulb, yet when it functions through the bulb, it looks as if it is the light. In fact, a lot of people use the word 'light' as a synonym for electricity.

When we see a piece of cloth, we do not see the cotton or silk that went into making it. But without cotton or silk, there would be no cloth. At the same time, a cloth cannot be called cotton or silk, it's called cloth only. Similarly, the consciousness is not the living beings themselves, but an unattached supporter of them all.

The human mind is governed by the three modes of nature, the rajas, sattva and tamas. Since it is the Self or the universal energy that functions as nature as well as soul, we can say that it is the modes of nature as well as the enjoyer of those modes, while remaining unattached to all.

SEPTEMBER

Day 1

He is inside as well as outside all beings, moving and unmoving. He is incomprehensible because of his subtlety. And because of his omnipresence, He is very near, residing in one's inner psyche, as well as far away in the Supreme Abode. (13.15)

The all-pervasiveness of Self or consciousness is explained here. Consciousness is like sound waves, which is present all around us in the air but audible to us only when we harness it through a radio. Although no activity is possible without consciousness, yet no one can see it or feel it. This is because of its subtle nature.

Since consciousness is all pervasive, it is actually unmoving. It is conditioned by the object through which it functions. So, when it is present in a moving being, we feel that consciousness is moving. It is like when we sit in a train, we are still. When the train moves, we move along with it, though we remain sitting.

Consciousness is present in our body, mind, intellect and also outside of these. It is a part of the universal energy, so we can say that consciousness is very near, in us, yet it is also far away as in the Supreme Abode.

Day 2

He is undivided and yet appears to exist as if divided in beings. He is the object of knowledge, and though appears as the sustainer, He is also the creator and destroyer of all beings. (13.16)

When the sun comes out, we see it from our window and say that the sun rose at this time. Thousands of miles away, in another country, the same thing happens, they also say that the sun rose at this time. That time is likely to be different from ours. But is the sun different? Or are there multiple suns? Everyone sees the same sun, though at different places.

Similarly, though the Self is seen in multiple beings, yet it is not divided.

Standing at the beach, we look at the sea and enjoy the sight of waves, rising up high, rushing towards the beach and then crashing down. Where do these waves come from and where do they go? They come from the sea and go back into the sea. The sea creates them, supports them and then devours them.

The Self too, creates the universe, sustains it and then annihilates it.

Day 3

The Supreme Being is the source of all light. He is beyond the darkness of ignorance. He is the Self-knowledge, the object of Self-knowledge and, seated in the inner psyche as consciousness of all beings, He is to be realized by Self-knowledge. (13.17)

The Supreme Being or super-soul is the light of wisdom. To see any object, we need to throw light on it. Likewise, to understand life and its experiences, we need wisdom. The light of wisdom by which we become aware of our own mental and intellectual states is the light of the super-soul or consciousness.

Where there is consciousness, there can be no darkness; where there is wisdom, ignorance doesn't exist. Hence consciousness or Self is said to transcend darkness.

The super-soul or Self is seated in the heart or inner psyche of all living beings as consciousness. It is the realization of this Self that is the goal of spiritual pursuit. When we control our senses, become detached and still our mind, we are ready to realize the Self. Once we focus single-pointedly on the Self, we realize it.

Day 4

Both the material nature and the Spiritual Being are beginning-less. All manifestations and three dispositions of mind and matter, called modes, are born of material nature. Material nature is responsible for production of physical body and organs of perception and action. Spiritual Being is responsible for experiencing pleasure and pain. (13.19-20)

Purush or Spiritual Being and prakriti or the material nature indicate two aspects of the same God or universal energy. Since the universal energy is causeless and eternal, its manifestations, purush and prakriti, are also beginning-less and endless.

Purush, the Spirit, is the inactive aspect in creation, while prakriti, the matter, is the kinetic aspect, the creator of the universe and beings. Their play causes the origin, preservation and dissolution of universe.

Prakriti or material nature is like the storm of maya or delusion that transforms the calm ocean of Spirit into tumultuous waves of living beings. The force of this storm comprises the three modes of manifestation.

As prakriti is responsible for creation of body and senses, purush is responsible for experiencing pleasure and pain caused by those senses, as it identifies with the body.

Day 5

Spiritual Being enjoys three modes of material nature by associating with them. Attachment to the three modes of nature due to ignorance caused by previous karma is the cause of birth of living entity in good and evil wombs. (13.21)

Since the Spiritual Being identifies with the physical body and the senses, it becomes the experiencer. It then experiences the qualities born of material nature, like heat and cold, pleasure and pain. And the trouble begins.

The Spiritual Being not only experiences the joys and sorrows of life, but also develops attachment with them. Such attachment is the cause of rebirth. The conditions of each new birth, whether good or evil, are directly related to the degree of the Spirit's attachment to the influences of the nature's good, active and evil modes. These modes are delusory and make the Spirit forget its real nature. This is termed as ignorance.

The rediscovery of its own real nature by the Spirit is only possible by removing ignorance through knowledge and removing attachments through dispassion.

Day 6

The Supreme Spirit or the super-soul in the body is the witness, the guide, the supporter, the enjoyer and the controller. (13.22)

Krishna mentions two purushs here, the lower Spirit and the higher Supreme Spirit. The lower one is the knower of the bodily field, the individual soul. The higher one is pure consciousness or the super-soul.

The super-soul is always with the individual soul and is the representation of God or universal energy. The individual soul enjoys the activities of the body, but the super-soul doesn't take part in the activities; it functions as a witness, overseer and permitter.

Without the sanction of super-soul, the individual soul cannot do anything. When it sees an evil action being performed, the super-soul is called a spectator or silent witness. When it sees a noble action being performed, it is called an approver. In other words, all activities of a person are indirectly witnessed by God.

Day 7

They who truly understand Spirit and the material nature with its three modes are not born again regardless of their way of life. (13.23)

Clear understanding of the material nature, individual soul and the super-soul and their inter-relationship makes one eligible to become free from the cycle of rebirths and merge with the universal energy.

Whether their position in life be high or low, whether or not they have acted according to the spiritual injunctions as perceived by society, Self-realized people are not subject to rebirth.

The purpose of Self-knowledge is to understand that the living being has, by chance, fallen into material existence and that one can revert to its source, if one tried sincerely.

Day 8

Some perceive the super-soul in their inner psyche through the mind and intellect that have been purified either by meditation or by metaphysical knowledge or by selfless service. (13.24)

The three main approaches to Self-realization are meditation (dhyana yoga), metaphysical knowledge (gyana yoga) and selfless service (karma yoga).

Meditation purifies the mind. Through meditation, the seeker withdraws his senses into his mind, not allowing them to run after their respective sensory temptations. Keeping it thus under control, the mind is directed towards the Self. These seekers become highly detached.

The path of metaphysical knowledge is for those who do not have the steadiness of mind and intellect. The study of scriptures and reflecting upon them leads the seeker to deeper conviction of the goal and the steadiness of mind to achieve it.

The path of selfless service is for those who are unable to study the scriptures due to their inner limitations. Such a seeker surrenders all his actions to God, renouncing the fruits of his actions. This produces purity of mind, leading to knowledge of Self.

Day 9

Others, however, do not know the yoga of meditation, knowledge and work, but they perform deity worship with faith, as mentioned in the scriptures by the saints and sages. They also transcend death by virtue of their firm faith on what they have heard. (13.25)

Listening to any spiritual master is an art, which can also lead the disciple to Self-realization. When a seeker knows nothing of meditation or metaphysical knowledge, nor can he dissociate himself from his work sufficiently, he can attain Self-realization by following his guru's teachings with full faith.

There are many people who listen to spiritual discourses and worship diligently, following the advice of their spiritual master. Then there are those who study spiritual books and faithfully adhere to the teachings contained in them. The goal is the same, whichever path one follows.

According to Krishna, it's faith that leads the seeker to transcend death.

Day 10

Whatever is born, animate or inanimate, know them to be born from the union of Spirit and matter. (13.26)

Whatever is created, be it animate or inanimate, is but a combination of the living entity Spirit and material nature or matter. Both Spirit and matter existed before the creation of cosmos. They are two aspects of the universal energy manifested for the purpose of creating the universe. Their relationship is eternal and is caused and controlled by their source, the universal energy, which is also eternal.

The union of Spirit and matter is not physical, but is of mutual superimposition. It is illusory. It is like the film projected on a blank screen from a projector. If the projector does not play, there is no film. If there is no blank screen to see the film on, then even if the projector plays, there would be no film to see. Both the projector and the screen are needed for the operator to show the film to the viewers.

The film itself is an illusion, a play of light. While it plays, it engrosses the viewers and creates all kinds of emotions in them. The emotions are real, the film is not. In fact, the emotions create an attachment in the viewer and he begins to love or hate the characters of the film. He then wants to see more films featuring the characters he loves.

The filmmakers sell illusions or dreams. Likewise, life as we see and experience is also a cosmic dream of God.

Day 11

The one who sees the same eternal Supreme Lord dwelling as Spirit equally within all mortal beings, truly sees. (13.27)

Most people live life very seriously. They sincerely believe that they need to do so much before they die. Guided or rather misguided by their senses, these people keep working towards satisfying their sensual needs. They create families and get busy in satisfying their family's sensual needs. They do not realize that a need is like a mirage in desert, it's there in front of you all the time but you can never reach it.

The reason why people are running all the time is because they see everything as different, which creates so many things for them to want and run after. The primary function of clothes used to be to cover and protect our body. Now that has become secondary. More than being need-based, clothes have become vanity-based. Same is true for food. What was once eaten to fulfil the body's need to grow and remain disease-free is now eaten to pamper the taste buds.

When we see through the mirage of our needs, we start seeing life differently. When we see that all the gold ornaments are made with the same gold, we start seeing fellow humans differently. When we recognize the changeless factor, the universal energy in everything, from the highest deity in temples to the grain of sand under our feet, we are in harmony with the universe.

Day 12

When one beholds one and the same Lord existing equally in every being, one does not injure anybody, because one considers everything as one's own Self. And thereupon attains the Supreme Abode. (13.28)

We always look after our own. Right from childhood, we have felt possessive about our belongings, be it our books, clothes, toys and gifts given by friends or family. As we grow older, our domain of possessions widens and includes our family and other material things. We look after them well, to the best of our capabilities.

We send our children to the best of schools, give them the best of food and clothes; if any of our loved ones falls sick, we get them the best of medical aid; we have annual maintenance contracts for our gadgets and insurances for our vehicles and other assets. In a nutshell, we really take care of our people and our possessions. Why? Because they are 'ours', we feel connected to them.

At a macro level, if we realize that every living being has the same universal energy or God in them as we do, then we would start looking at them differently. They would seem to us as our own. There would be no petty fights or wars then, as we would not like to hurt our own.

Day 13

The one who perceives that all work is done by the powers of material nature, truly understands, and thus does not consider oneself as the doer. (13.29)

We want to possess things that we think we need. Most of the time, for most of the things, it's the producer of those things who, through excellent marketing, has convinced us that we need what they are selling. It's all emotional, and the emotions are created by our senses. So, it boils down to the fact that we are controlled by our senses.

The wise step back a little from the material world and observe themselves. They see that most of their needs are not their needs at all, they are the needs of their senses. They don't need the latest model of mobile phone, the earlier one is functioning just fine. They don't need a larger TV, nor do they need a bigger car and so on and so forth. They can see how their senses get tempted and trap them into acquiring unnecessary things. They decide to take control in their own hands.

With the help of their intellect, such people are able to control their senses and detach themselves from the material world.

Day 14

The moment one discovers diverse variety of beings and their different ideas abiding in One, and coming out from That alone, one attains the Supreme Being. (13.30)

The people who have recently discovered their diabetes, try their best to avoid sweets. For them, food that are less sweet, moderately sweet or more sweet, are the same. They are sweet, and they have to avoid them. This is a very gross example, but the idea is to be alert about the composition of things around us.

The animal lovers, especially pet-owners, can vouch for the fact that animals feel the same way as humans, and behave even better. The plant lovers would swear to plants having feelings. It has been seen that indoor plants wither if the inmates of the house are loud and aggressive; the same plants flourish in peaceful environs.

The wise see this and realize that all living beings have the same soul. Even in humans, the stature they hold in society is superficial. At the level of the soul, all humans are the same.

Day 15

Because of being beginning-less and unaffectable by the three modes of material nature, the eternal super-soul, even though dwelling in the body as a living entity, neither does anything nor becomes tainted. Just as the all-pervading space is not tainted because of its subtlety, similarly, the Spirit abiding in all bodies is not tainted. (13.31–13.32)

The individual soul carries with it various leftover desires from its past life. It takes birth in a new body to fulfil them, the body being the field of play for the individual soul.

The material nature of body is governed by the three modes:

sattva (goodness), rajas (passion) and tamas (ignorance), which dictate all thoughts and actions and bind the individual soul to the body. The cycle of cause and effect continues, the cause creating the effect and the effect giving rise to another cause.

Meanwhile, the universal energy, which is the source and cause of the individual soul and the body, pervades it in the form of the super-soul. This super-soul functions as a neutral observer, unaffected by the modes of nature and the action-interaction of individual soul and the body. Just as space remains unaffected by the various galaxies it contains, so the super-soul remains untainted by the bodies it inhabits.

Day 16

They who perceive, with the eye of Self-knowledge, the difference between the body (matter) and the knower of the body (Spirit), as well as know the technique of liberation of the living entity from the trap of divine illusory energy (maya), attain the Supreme. (13.34)

Krishna concludes that a human being's life is fulfilled only when his individual soul (Spirit) merges with its source, the super-soul or Self. This is called Self-realization.

The way to Self-realization is to control the senses and meditate upon the constitution of the body, the individual soul and the super-soul and their relationship with each other. An understanding of this will lead the seekers to discover the super-soul within themselves and break out from the trap of material delusion.

The study of scriptures and teachings of spiritual masters also help the seekers reach their spiritual goal of Self-realization.

14

Three Qualities of Material Nature

17–30 September

Day 17

My womb of creation is the material nature wherein I place the seed of my intelligence. This is the cause of the birth of all beings. (14.03)

Krishna tells Arjun how he is the father and also the mother of the universe. Matter and Spirit are two aspects of the universal energy, Krishna. These aspects are inherent in the energy mass and are manifested when Krishna wants to create the universe.

As father, Krishna places the seed of his intelligence, the Spirit, into the womb, which is material nature or matter. This union results in the production of the cosmic egg. All the beings in the universe are created from this egg.

The Spirit carries the blueprint of all future births, which happen to depend on its interaction with the three modes of nature. It also carries intelligence, which is the power of discrimination, to distinguish the right from the wrong.

Material nature is also addressed as Mother nature, as it is seen as giving birth to the entire creation. But since material nature is also an aspect of Krishna, it is actually Krishna who is the real mother.

Day 18

Goodness sattva, rajas and tamas—with these three modes or ropes, material nature fetters the eternal individual soul to the body. (14.05)

Goodness, passion and ignorance, the three modes of material nature are always present in all human beings. However, they are never constant. At any given point of time, only one out of the three dominates. Under the influence of the three modes of nature, our mind expresses itself in a variety of ways at different moments of changing environments.

When the individual soul identifies with the body, it gets trapped by the modes of nature. Accordingly, it feels the changes in the body as its own changes and becomes subject to the joys and sorrows of the body. This is called delusion; the soul forgets its own reality.

Day 19

The mode of goodness attaches one to happiness of learning and knowing the Spirit, the mode of passion attaches to action and the mode of ignorance attaches to negligence by covering the Self-knowledge. (14.09)

A person in the mode of goodness is satisfied by their work or intellectual pursuit, just as a philosopher, scientist or an educator may be engaged in a particular field of knowledge and may be satisfied in that way.

A person in the mode of passion is habitually engaged in worldly activities. Passion gives birth to thirst and attachment. A passionate person owns as much as they can and spend for good causes.

The mode of ignorance covers right judgment and knowledge. An ignorant person is steeped in misconceptions and errors. In this mode, whatever one does is neither good for them, nor for others.

Day 20

Goodness prevails by suppressing passion and ignorance; passion prevails by suppressing goodness and ignorance and ignorance prevails by suppressing goodness and passion. (14.10)

Do the three modes of nature act on our mind all at one time or each separately at different points of time?

According to Krishna, these modes are acting on our mind all the time. But at any given point of time, human personality works under the influence of one predominant mode, while the other two are subdued, but never totally absent.

When the mode of goodness is prominent, passion and ignorance are defeated and the mind is filled with feelings of happiness. When the mode of passion is prominent, goodness and ignorance are defeated and the mind is filled with desires, actions and attachments. When the mode of ignorance is prominent, passion and goodness are defeated and the mind becomes unaware of its nobler duties. The competition is always on.

Day 21

When the light of Self-knowledge makes all the senses in the body glitter, then it should be known that goodness is predominant. (14.11)

The sense organs, through which the body receives stimuli from the external, material world are termed as the gates of the body. Through these gates the light of awareness enters us and illuminates us from inside.

When there is unruffled peace of mind, inner harmony, absolute tranquillity, clarity of vision and penetrative insight, then we should understand that sattva or goodness predominates.

When goodness is predominant, the ears refuse to hear improper sounds, the eyes will not see undesirable sights, the tongue avoids saying anything improper and the mind is not attracted towards sensual objects. Increase in sattva results in increase of knowledge and increase of wisdom.

Day 22

When passion is predominant, greed, activity, undertaking of selfish works, restlessness and excitement arise. (14.12)

People who are in a predominant mode of passion are never satisfied with whatever position they are in life; they hanker for more. Such people are full of greed, which leads to selfish activity.

Selfish activities carry a lot of expectations and associated anxiety with them. Engrossed in fears of loss, these people are always restless. They are so busy running after sense fulfilment that they can never really enjoy life. They are always too exhausted.

The only positive side to this mode of nature is that such people support themselves and their family. They are not a burden on anyone. In fact, such passionate people help society by doing charitable work. It's a good way to expend their surplus energy.

Day 23

When inertia is predominant; ignorance, inactivity, carelessness and delusion arise. (14.13)

Where there is no illumination, knowledge is absent. One in a predominant mode of ignorance acts whimsically, for no purpose. Even though they have the capacity, they make no effort to work.

Ignorance is a state of darkness in which one's intellect is unable to arrive at any decision. The person is beset with inertness and lacks enthusiasm to achieve anything in the world. This state of mind also makes the person incapable of discerning good from bad, and creates havoc in their relationships.

Ignorant people fail to understand the world and live in a

permanent state of delusion. They eventually become a burden to society.

Day 24

They who are established in goodness go to heaven; passionate persons are reborn in the mortal world; and the insipid ones, abiding in the mode of ignorance, go to lower planets of hell, or take birth as lower creatures, depending on the degree of their ignorance. (14.18)

This verse is about the continuity of existence after death. Those who are living a pure life of discrimination, clear thinking, right judgement and self-discipline, cultivate more and more goodness in themselves. When the mind is thus quiet, it evolves to a higher level. Such people go to heaven. Heaven is the place where Brahma resides.

The mode of passion is mixed; it is in the middle of goodness and ignorance. A passionate person will return to earth as a rich person or a king/queen. But if there is a slight leaning towards ignorance, then the person has the chance of becoming mad in the next life. Normally, being full of desires and ambitions, the passionate person would continue to come back as a human to finish what they had left unfinished.

Ignorance is the lowest quality and leads the person to hell. Ignorant people are full of misconceptions and delusions. Depending on their level of delusions, they devolve into lower species of life like birds, reptiles, trees and so on.

Day 25

When visionaries perceive no doer other than the powers of the Supreme Being in the modes of material nature; and know That which is above and beyond these modes, then they attain nirvana or salvation. (14.19)

One can transcend all the activities of the modes of material nature simply by understanding them properly.

A wise person understands when they are watching a movie that it is created with the help of a beam of light falling through a variegated film on to a screen. Similarly, a yogi also understands that the phenomena of the material world is a play of the three modes of nature, animated by the light of the universal energy.

With the help of meditation, the yogi transcends his own mind and intellect to discover that the modes of nature transform themselves into bodies, senses and sense objects, and that the Supreme Consciousness is higher than the modes of nature. He also discovers the Consciousness reflected in his mind as the individual soul. He realizes that he himself was the cause of his delusion. This wise man would be considered as Self-realized.

Day 26

When one rises above the three modes of material nature that originate in the body, one attains immortality or salvation, and is freed from the pains of birth, old age, and death. (14.20)

The joys and sorrows that we go through in life—the pains of birth, old age and death—are actually experienced by our body. They are caused by three modes of nature. When we identify with our body, we also identify with the modes of nature and all that goes along with them.

As children, when we fell and scraped our knee, the sight of blood made us cry. Then our mothers picked us up and distracted our attention from the injury by showing us how many ants we killed by falling over them. This technique has always worked with us as children. But what happens when we grow up? We become body-conscious and hence hurt more. It's all in the mind, after all.

Once we get a grip on our emotions, and stop being sensitive to everything and everyone around us, we would realize that our sorrows have reduced. This is at a very basic level, but proves the point anyway. For a long-term solution, meditation is the answer.

Deep, intense meditation helps us to go beyond physical consciousness and thus beyond the three modes of nature that influence us. At that level, we experience the infinite supreme consciousness, which is immortal. This is Self-realization.

Day 27

One who neither hates the presence of peace, activity and confusion, nor desires for them when they are absent, who remains like a witness without being affected by the modes of material nature and stays firmly attached to the Lord without wavering, thinking that the modes of material nature only are operating, is the one who has transcended the modes of nature. (14.22–14.23)

People normally tend to get affected by their surroundings. The noisy late-night party of a neighbour, the smelly feet of a co-passenger in flight, the short-tempered boss and many more varied situations can spoil their day.

There are two ways to deal with such issues. First one is to tell the person concerned and hope they won't take offense and act on resolving the issue. This method may not always be successful, as it banks on the other person. The second way is to ignore the issue completely. It is not difficult to inculcate this habit. They just need to remember their childhood, how they were told to ignore their injury so as not to feel its pain.

The wise know that people behave under the influence of their own mode of nature. They cannot control them. They can only control their reactions to them. This is the true realization of Self.

Day 28

The one who lives in the Self and is indifferent to pain and pleasure; to whom a clod, a stone and gold are alike; to whom the dear and the unfriendly are alike; who is of firm mind, who is calm in censure and in praise, is said to have transcended the modes of material nature. (14.24)

We can learn how to ignore irritation or pain, but that's not enough. We need to learn to ignore pleasure as well, which is a tough call. Nobody wants to be in pain, so it is easy enough to train yourself to ignore it. But everyone wants pleasure; why would they want to ignore it? Because pleasure creates greed; we want more and more of it. Greed is an overwhelming desire that traps the best of people.

The wise know this fact and steer away from feeling any intense emotion, be it pain or pleasure, heat or cold. For them, a ring made of copper is no different from that made of gold, as both serve the same purpose. Such people consider no one as their enemy, as everyone is equally dear to them.

They are indifferent to blame or praise, and are secure in themselves and their work. Such a person, who maintains equanimity in all circumstances, is said to have transcended the modes of material nature.

Day 29

The one who is indifferent to honour and disgrace, who is impartial to friend and foe, and who has renounced the sense of doership, is said to have transcended the modes of material nature. (14.25)

One of the clear signs of equanimity is remaining unruffled in the face of honour or disgrace. These social, and sometimes personal, evaluations by people keep changing from time to time. A wise person knows this. They have already crossed over the planes of egoism and vanity. Roses and thorns are the same to them.

When we indulge in any activity for a personal reason, to satisfy our desires or ego, we consider ourselves to be the doer of the same. This is attachment and creates expectation of desired result, happiness on getting it, and disappointment at not getting it.

The wise do not get entangled in such a situation. They work selflessly, renouncing any attachment to the work or its fruit. Such people have transcended the modes of material nature and are said to be Self-realized.

Day 30

The one who offers service to me with love and unswerving devotion, transcends three modes of material nature and becomes fit for nirvana, or salvation. (14.26)

Contemplation on anything with utmost sincerity helps us in getting it. This is the law of attraction, the secret of manifestation. We are taught from childhood to focus single-pointedly on our goal and work towards it, like target shooting or running or any other sport where the focus is to win.

Many times, our minds may not always be completely free of thoughts. This is true especially for people who lead a full life working and looking after family as well. Such situations need reinforcements.

Krishna suggests that selfless service, devoting the fruits of action to God, is a form of worship. It can be done all the time for all our actions. The result is that we are constantly remembering God instead of wasting time on thinking about the results of our various actions. This makes it easier for us to meditate, as our mind would be less agitated now. The chances of our achieving the goal of Self-realization become brighter.

15

Realization of the Ultimate Truth

1–11 October

OCTOBER

Day 1

The universe (or human body) may be compared to an eternal tree that has its origin (or root) in the Supreme Being and its branches below in the cosmos. The Vedic hymns are the leaves of this tree. One who understands this tree is a knower of the vedas. (15.01)

Krishna tells Arjun about the eternal cosmic tree that has its root above and branches below. It is like an upside down peepal tree.

The root arises from the Supreme Being or God as he is the source of all beings. The branches are the desires, from which sprout the shoots of action that give rise to desire once again, in an endless cycle. The colourful and fragrant flowers and fruits grow and bloom, but eventually they wither or rot and die.

The millions of leaves seen on the branches are meant as protection and denote the vedas, the words of wisdom. The knower of tree is also the knower of the vedas.

As the branches reach closer to earth, they plunge in and become roots from which new trees arise. Gradually a forest develops around the cosmic tree.

The cosmic tree is reflected in the human body as our nervous system. From the brain as the source, the nerves branch down to each part of the body, right up to our toes.

Day 2

The branches of this eternal tree are spread all over the cosmos. The tree is nourished by the energy of material nature; sense pleasures are its sprouts and its roots of ego and desires stretch below in the human world, causing karmic bondage. (15.02)

The branches of the eternal cosmic tree spread all over, upward and downward. The upward growing branches denote evolution of some individual souls. But most branches grow downward and enter the earth, giving rise to roots and more trees. They denote the basal tendency of the souls influenced by the material nature.

The tendency to lead a higher or lower form of life is determined by the dominance of one of the three modes of nature.

The roots that arise from the branches entering the earth are the secondary roots, the main being the original one in the cosmos. The secondary roots are the ego, attaching the tree firmly into the earth, denoting karmic attachments that bind the soul to the material nature.

Day 3

The beginning, the end, or the real form of this tree is not perceptible on the earth. Having cut the firm roots (the desires) of this tree by the mighty axe of Self-knowledge and detachment, one should seek that Supreme Abode from where one does not come back to the mortal world again. (15.03–15.04)

The branches (of desire) of this cosmic tree grow thick and hard and plunge into the earth. They put down roots there and become giant trees themselves. After some time, a forest grows around the main cosmic tree. It seems that the forest has sprung up from the earth. The cosmic tree gets hidden from sight.

This analogy denotes our state in the material world. The tree constantly grows as that is its nature. The branches of desires continue to spread, some of them taking deep roots and resulting in producing more desires. When we desire a big house, the story doesn't end there. We then need to fill it up, which results in desiring more things. It goes on, forever.

Surrounded by an ever-growing jungle of desires, we lose sight of the cosmic tree, the stem or trunk of which denotes the individual soul. The sap running through the tree, giving it life and consciousness, is Krishna or the super-soul.

In order to reach the trunk of the cosmic tree, we have to cut down the forest of desires with the axe of detachment. We must remember at all times that the goal of our soul is to merge with the source.

Day 4

Those who are free from pride and delusion, who have conquered the evil of attachment, who are constantly dwelling in the Supreme Being, with all lust completely stilled, who are free from dualities of pleasure and pain, such wise ones reach my Supreme Abode. (15.05)

Krishna explains to Arjun certain disciplines, following which one could lead a life of fulfilment.

The first step is to free oneself from pride. Pride leads to erroneous judgment and delusion. People develop a false sense of importance and arrogance, which preoccupies their thoughts so much that they ignore the greater values of life. The next step is to drop attachments. Since detachment is not very easy, it's better to divert the attachment to God.

The most important discipline is to still the mind. Once the senses are controlled, stilling of the mind becomes easier. Then one also becomes free of the dualities of material nature like pleasure and pain. In this state of equanimity, one is able to commune with Self and attain Supreme Abode. The spiritual purpose of life is thus fulfilled.

Day 5

The individual soul in the body of living beings is the integral part of the universal Spirit or consciousness. The individual soul associates with the six sensory faculties (including the mind) of perception and activates them. (15.07)

If God is the ocean, then humans are the wave. As human beings are a part of God, they are never really away from him.

The vast sky becomes a small square-shaped sky when reflected in a square-shaped bowl. Likewise, the Spirit of God becomes differently displayed—as is the individual soul—in different human beings and other living creatures. As the little sky reflected in the vessel is no different in essence from the vast sky, so the infinite Spirit of God, reflected as the individual soul in all the beings, is same in essence.

The power of seeing, hearing, etc., is the power of the universal Spirit functioning through the sense organs. The six senses, the five external ones and the mind, therefore, are the soul's instruments of communication with the world.

Day 6

Just as the air takes aroma away from the flower, similarly, the individual soul takes the six sensory faculties from the physical body it casts off during death to the new physical body it acquires in reincarnation. (15.08)

After the death of a person, the individual soul transmigrates into another person. Its last body and its activities are the background for the soul's next body. The soul gets the body according to its karma.

The individual soul is also considered as the Lord as it is the ruler of the body, regulating all actions, feelings and thoughts. If it wants, it can change its body to a higher class or to a lower one.

Just as the wind takes away the scent from its source, the flowers, so in death the individual soul moves off, taking with it all sensory faculties, including the mind and the intellect. Then, as and when it wants, the soul enters another new body.

Day 7

The living entity enjoys sense pleasures using six sensory faculties of hearing, touch, sight, taste, smell and mind. The ignorant cannot perceive the living entity departing from the body or staying in the body and enjoying sense pleasures by associating with the material body. But those who have the eye of Self-knowledge can see it. (15.09-10)

The individual soul enjoys the material world through sense organs and the mind. The consciousness reflects upon mind and intellect and becomes intelligence, with which the sense organs become illuminated. The individual soul, using the mind along with sense organs, enjoys the sense objects such as sound, touch, taste, smell, etc.

Consciousness is originally pure, like water. But if we add any colour to water, it changes. Similarly, consciousness also changes according to its association with material qualities, which results in its getting the appropriate body in its subsequent life. It means, if the individual soul adulterates its consciousness with qualities of dogs, in its next life, it gets the body of a dog.

An ignorant person's perceptions are covered over by the veil of the modes of nature, and hence they can't perceive the individual soul or Self. Only those with the inner eye of knowledge can see it.

Day 8

I am seated in the inner psyche of all beings. The memory, Self-knowledge, and the removal of doubts about God come from me. I am that which is to be known by the study of all the vedas. I am, indeed, the author as well as the student of the vedas. (15.15)

God is life, mind, senses, soul and ego in man. He is also the power of feeling in the heart, which determines the way human beings react to their contact with the objects of the senses.

God empowers memory, by which perceptions and cognitions are gathered and held together to be connected with one another in accumulation of knowledge.

God is the essence of all knowledge; he is the source of all wisdom in the vedas. The seeker who listens to the vedas, reflects on their wisdom and who finally experiences the fulfilment of his life, is also considered as nothing other than consciousness. So, God is the knowledge and the knower.

Day 9

There are two entities in the cosmos: the changeable Temporal Beings, and the unchangeable Eternal Being (Spirit). All created beings are subject to change, but the Spirit does not change. (15.16)

The two entities in the cosmos are perishable and imperishable. Anything changeable, which includes the entire existence, is considered as perishable. The living beings that are struggling in this world, with their mind and five senses, have material bodies that are constantly changing.

In the material world, the living entity undergoes six changes: birth, growth, existence, reproduction, dwindling and vanishing. These are changes of the material body, but the individual soul or the Spirit does not change.

The Spirit is like the anvil that is used to shape iron products.

Hot iron becomes malleable and is placed on the anvil and beaten into the desired shape, like a horseshoe, a vessel, etc. All the while, when the iron is hammered, the anvil remains changeless, though it plays an important role in the shaping of iron.

So, matter is changeable and perishable, while the Spirit remains unchangeable and imperishable.

Day 10

The Supreme Being is beyond both the Temporal and the Eternal Beings. He is also called the Absolute Reality that sustains both the Temporal and the Eternal by pervading everything. (15.17)

We may have reached the highest rung in the corporate ladder, we may be the CEO of our company, but after some time we would retire. For years, decades even, we enjoy running the company, we enjoy the power we had, the control we had over the working of a big organization. But when it all goes away, do we cease to exist? When our designation is taken away from us, do we lose our identity too?

People who go into severe depression after retirement are the ones who identify themselves with the post they held. But they also come back to the reality soon enough. The reality is our individuality.

At a macro level, matter or material nature is considered the field and Spirit or individual soul is considered as the knower of the field. The knower of the field is 'knower' because of the field. If we take away the field, what happens to the knower? He is not a knower any more, but he still exists. As what? The knower now is the 'knowing principle' or just knowledge.

When the perishable is no more and the imperishable is no more, what is left is only energy. It is the universal energy that was the essence of both. This energy is pure consciousness or the Supreme Being.

Day 11

Because the Supreme Being is beyond both Temporal and Eternal, therefore, he is known in this world and in the scriptures as the Supreme Being (absolute reality, truth, super-soul) (15.18)

According to Carl Jung, 'The word happiness would lose its meaning if it were not contrasted and compared to sadness.'[6] If we look around us, we find that we live in a world of opposites. There is no way to explain light without darkness, or wetness without dryness. Without first creating a parameter to compare with, we cannot use the terms, fat, thin, tall or short.

Therefore, the perishable matter also seems to change only against the imperishable truth, as no change can be perceptible without reference to a changeless factor.

When we build a pot and put water in it, we have created the terms 'inside' and 'outside'. We say there is water inside the pot, and there is no water outside the pot. Where there is no pot, there is no inside or outside.

We have seen that the perishable matter and the imperishable Spirit carry the essence of the universal energy. When they are no more, only energy remains. As this universal energy is superior to all beings, perishable and imperishable, it is known as the Supreme Being.

---

[6]Sreechinth C., *The Musings of Carl Jung*, UB Tech, 2018, p. 132.

16

Divine and the Demonic Natures

12–18 October

Day 12

Fearlessness, purity of inner psyche, perseverance in the yoga of Self-knowledge, charity, sense-restraint, sacrifice, study of the scriptures, austerity, honesty, non-violence, truthfulness, equanimity, compassion for all creatures, absence of malice and absence of pride, these are some of the qualities of those endowed with divine virtues. (16.01–16.03)

This is a list of good qualities that lead a devotee to Self-realization. Fear causes mental, physical and spiritual disturbances in a person. Extreme fright is known to have caused heart failure. Long-continued fears give rise to chronic nervousness, eventually manifesting as physical disease. All this happens because fear ties us, our soul, to our material self.

Attachment to anything, as we know, gives rise to fear of losing it. Fearlessness, for a devotee, is his undaunted faith in God, his love, wisdom, justice, mercy and protection. A fearless man's soul is free from his material body's shackles.

Once the mind is turned inwards, it can renounce worldly desires and attain purity. This, in turn, is achieved by yoga and steadfast devotion to acquiring knowledge of scriptures.

Charity here means sharing of knowledge. Whatever we have should be shared with fellow beings. When one has all these major good qualities along with freedom from self-importance, one becomes spiritually richer and closer to God.

Day 13

The marks of those who are born with demonic qualities are hypocrisy, arrogance, pride, anger, harshness and ignorance. (16.04)

Self-importance makes people delusional and unaware of reality. Such people believe that having money or social status or even bookish knowledge is a sign of their greatness. They would then arrogantly demean others to make themselves look grander.

There is no limit to the harsh behaviour of these self-centred, egoistical people. Desiring to always have things their own way, they are prone to anger and aggression, often leading to violence. They have their own distorted sense of values for their own selves, which are completely different from what they have for others. Full of hypocrisy, they have lost the sense of discrimination of right from wrong.

Krishna named such nature of a person as devilish or demonic.

Day 14

Divine qualities lead to salvation; the demonic qualities are said to be for bondage. Do not grieve, you are born with divine qualities. (16.05)

Learning about the good and the devilish qualities would make anyone wonder which category they fall into. It is like when we start reading about various diseases on the internet, we suddenly find, to our utter dismay and fear, that most of the disease symptoms are present in us.

Arjun felt the same. But Krishna assured him that his nature was inherently good and not demonic.

Arjun's involvement in the war was not demonic, as he was not acting under anger, pride, arrogance or ignorance. For any warrior, fighting is not demonic, it is his duty. Any casualties of war are collateral damage.

According to Krishna, a divine or good-natured person is liberated from mental entanglements by living a life of righteousness. On the other hand, a demonic nature leads the person to confusion and a sorrowful life.

Day 15

Lust, anger and greed are the three gates of hell leading to the downfall (or bondage) of the individual. Therefore, one must learn to give up these three. (16.21)

Lust, anger and greed are the basest of emotions that bind people to the material world so strongly that they are unable to get out easily.

Lust means a strong desire for anything, whether it is sexual pleasure, food, money, amassing property or any other material goods. When lust is not fulfilled for any reason, it results in anger; stronger the desire, stronger the anger. Anger leads to violence. As can be seen, it's a downward spiral.

If people are able to gratify their lust, it makes them happy briefly, and then greed sets in. They want more. This goes on like a vicious cycle. The desires always have a tendency to grow in quantum as well as intensity. We desire for good clothes, which increases to wanting the latest in vogue by the best of designers, and to getting them custom made, and so on. We may spend a fortune on our clothes and yet be not satisfied.

The people who are entrapped in these three emotions of lust, anger and greed continue to be reborn to fulfil their endless desires. Their individual soul devolves, leading to their downfall to lives each worse than the previous. Hence these emotions are termed as gates of hell.

Day 16

One who is liberated from these three gates of hell, does what is best for him or her, and consequently attains the Supreme Abode. (16.22)

The solution to a problem begins by identifying the problem. Once we are able to identify the three emotions of lust, anger and greed in ourselves, we have to try to control them.

We need to be alert. The moment we are beset by anger, instead of reacting immediately, we should pause. This pause is not to count from one to ten so that our anger dissipates; it is to ask ourselves what is the cause behind our anger. We should not allow the anger to control us. If we do this exercise often enough, we would see a decrease in our anger levels.

Greed is easier to control. We need to be alert about when we are acquiring more than what we require. Once we are conscious of that, we can easily stop ourselves from getting swayed by greed. Since greed stems from lust, controlling it would dilute the intensity of lust too, till it dies its own death.

Having abandoned these three gates of hell, we would be heading in the right direction, towards the Supreme Abode.

Day 17

One who acts under the influence of his or her desires, disobeying scriptural injunctions, neither attains perfection nor happiness, nor the Supreme Abode. (16.23)

Computer or any other electronic device, any machine or an electrical gadget, comes with a how-to-do manual—so does life. The scriptures are the manuals telling us how to live life correctly, so that we get the best out of it.

When we start operating any machine or gadget as per our whim or fancy, instead of following its manual, it is bound to result in a disaster. Imagine driving a car on the road without knowing how to drive!

If we have read the manual but do not want to follow it—well, the result would still be the same. It is like taking the prescription for a disease from a doctor and not following it. The disease would never get cured.

Just as we take care of our physical and mental health, we should take care of our spiritual health too. According to Krishna, if we do not follow the scriptures, which are the life-manuals, we would live a restless life, full of agitations and sorrow.

Day 18

Let the scriptures be your authority in determining what should be done and what should not be done. You should perform your duty following the scriptural injunction. (16.24)

The human body is a miniature universe within the larger universe, both having the same underlying universal intelligence or consciousness. The same cosmic powers that create and govern the macrocosm of the universe, are also at work in man, the microcosm.

According to Krishna, the goal of human existence is to become re-established in one's true Self, the soul. Whatever is created has to go back to its source, to be created again, like clay is recycled to create pots and gold is recycled to create ornaments.

The path to Self-realization is explained in the scriptures. But mere reading does not give us knowledge, it just gives us theoretical information. Real knowledge is in the practical application of theoretical information.

Without knowledge, we are bound to commit mistakes and get stuck in the mortal material world, suffering with every birth. The only way out is to follow the scriptural instructions with utmost sincerity.

17

Threefold Faith

19 October–12 November

Day 19

The faith of one is in accordance with one's own natural disposition that is governed by karmic impressions. A person is known by the faith. One can become whatever one wants to be, if one constantly contemplates on the object of desire with faith. (17.03)

Faith is belief, and everyone has different belief systems that they follow. The faith of a person stems from his basic nature—sattvic or divine, rajasic or passionate and tamasic or diabolic. This basic nature of the person is based on the karmic impressions from their previous life.

Our predominant mode of nature governs our faith, which in turn governs our view of life, which conditions our desires, thoughts and actions.

If a person's innate tendencies are characterised by sattva, then their faith would direct them in the pursuit of knowledge and happiness. If their tendencies are governed by rajas, they would be directed towards the pursuit of action, ending in pain and suffering. If characterized by tamas, the faith would lead the person to ignorance and delusion.

Clearly, a person is made of their faith, and the intensity of their faith accounts for their passion in pursuing any task.

Day 20

Persons in the mode of goodness worship celestial controllers; those in the mode of passion worship supernatural rulers and demons; and those in the mode of ignorance worship ghosts and spirits. (17.04)

According to Krishna, a person's religion is not demonstrated by his formal path of worship, but by his mode of nature. Everyone lives according to the laws of their own nature. Therefore, they follow one of the three paths of worship.

A sattvic or good person worships the gods for their own sake, seeking nothing but their blessings. Their joy is in the act of worship itself; their worship is selfless as are their other actions in life.

A rajasic or passionate person worships gods related to wealth and power. Their idea of worship is based on desire and greed; they offer gifts to gods in return for fulfilment of their material desires.

A tamasic or ignorant person worships the spirits of the dead and various other ghosts. Such a person can be seen worshipping trees and graves. As we can see, our path of worship is also based on our faith, our belief system.

Day 21

They who practise severe austerities without following the prescription of the scriptures; who are full of hypocrisy and egotism; who are impelled by the forces of desire and attachment; who senselessly torture the elements in their body and also me who dwells within their body; know these ignorant persons to be of demonic nature. (17.05–17.06)

There are people who have manufactured modes of austerity and penance, which are mentioned nowhere in any scriptures. Some even commit acts of violence on their own bodies, like piercing it with needles, denying themselves food and water, walking barefoot for miles on stony paths, taking dips in icy cold rivers in extreme winters, etc.

These misguided people confuse self-torture with faith and devotion. They don't realize that they are actually showing disrespect to the elements that sustain their body, including their soul, which is the essence of God.

Some do it out of genuine ignorance and others indulge in such behaviour to gain admiration from people. This show of egotism constitutes a demonic nature.

Day 22

The food preferred by all of us is also of three types. So are the sacrifice, austerity and charity. (17.07)

As faith differs according to the mode of nature of a person, so does his food preferences. In fact, a person's attitude towards anything and everything in life, reflects their mode of nature. Their attitude to offering worship to God, their attitude to penance and their attitude to charity also mark a person as one of three types of people: sattvic, rajasic or tamasic.

One who offers their every action to God, expecting nothing in return; who believes that any work of theirs is a sacred duty and is detached from its fruit; whose every action is selfless, where they have nothing to gain; such a person is of sattvic nature

One who carries out any sacrifice keeping in mind what they would gain for themself from it; who performs actions to gain admiration and appreciation from others or as a display of their own power or wealth, such a person is of rajasic nature. One who acts without thinking; who does not care how their actions would affect others; who doesn't follow any rules, such a person is of tamasic nature.

Day 23

The foods that promote longevity, virtue, strength, health, happiness and joy are juicy, smooth, substantial and nutritious. Persons in the mode of goodness like such foods. (17.08)

What we eat has physical as well as mental consequences. The body cells are built with food and the mind is also affected by the nature of food. The three modes of material nature apply to foods as well.

Sattvic foods are sweet, fresh fruits and vegetables, whole grains and legumes, fresh dairy products, nuts, natural sweets like dates, honey and jaggery, and minimal amounts of fat. The foods are cooked to enhance their nutrients, are pleasing to the eye, tasteful and easy to digest.

A sattvic diet promotes good health, vitality and longevity. It also works on the mind and makes it calm, contented, cheerful and spiritually inclined. Persons in the mode of goodness naturally gravitate towards a sattvic diet regime.

Day 24

Foods that are very bitter, sour, salty, hot, pungent, dry and burning and cause pain, grief and disease are liked by persons in the mode of passion. (17.09)

Rajasic foods stimulate the life forces of our body, including our mind and senses. Stimulants are not always bad. In fact, for an average materially active person, they might be helpful to some degree.

Rajasic foods include bitter, sour, salty, spicy, pungent foods that are exciting to the tongue but disagreeable to the system. Eggs are considered rajasic, as well as fish and fowl.

These foods should be taken in moderation as they tend to cause acidity and disturbed sleep, eventually leading to various diseases. On the whole, they are irritating to both body and mind and result in mental agitation and distress. People with rajasic temperament enjoy this kind of food as it enhances their passions.

Day 25

The foods liked by people in the mode of ignorance are stale, tasteless, putrid, rotten and impure. (17.10)

Tamasic foods are essentially unhygienic and stale. Improper preparation or preservation can turn sattvic or rajasic food into tamasic. The most naturally tamasic foods are meats of higher forms of life like beef, pork and mutton.

Unhygienically prepared street food, rotten fruits and vegetables, pest-infested grains, contaminated food and water, stale mouldy foods are some of the commonly available tamasic foods.

A tamasic diet taken for long term has a malignant effect on the body and dulls the mind.

Day 26

Selfless service, enjoined by the scriptures, and performed without the desire for the fruit, with a firm belief and conviction that it is a duty, is in the mode of goodness. (17.11)

Most people go to temples or other religious shrines only when they need something in life. Someone prays to get admission in the college of their choice, someone prays to get a job, some pray for the health of their loved ones and so on. This kind of service to God is not in the mode of goodness.

One should go to the temple or any other religious shrine as a matter of duty and offer selfless service. Services like feeding the hungry, giving clothes to the needy, educating the under-privileged, etc., should be done without any selfish motive. The motive should be only to help those who need our help. This is the sattvic way to serve God.

Day 27

Service that is performed only for show, and aiming for fruit, know that to be in the mode of passion. (17.12)

People conduct elaborate prayer services, inviting hundreds of people to watch or participate. Spending that kind of money serves no purpose, except to show off the wealth of the host. People who attend such ostentatious ceremonies do not bless the host—they just eat, observe and pass comments on the show of wealth.

Some people try to make a deal with God. They build temples or install expensive idols in return for some major favour they ask of God. Do they really believe that God could be bribed? Or that God operates out of greed? This is sheer ignorance. This kind of selfish service is termed as rajasic.

Day 28

Service that is performed without following the scriptures, in which no food is distributed, which is devoid of mantra, faith and gift, is said to be in the mode of ignorance. (17.13)

Normally, a prayer service or worship of any god or goddess requires a priest. A priest is professionally trained to perform the rituals appropriate for the worship. After the service is concluded, the priest is paid his fee or given a gift as a token of gratitude. The people attending the service are fed clean sattvic food. The atmosphere is of prayer and devotion.

On the other hand, there are some people who do not follow the scriptures and perform voodoo-like practices. Their gods are spirits of departed people, which could be living in a tree or a rock. Such services are conducted at night as that's the time when spirits and demons are most active. This kind of delusional service is considered tamasic.

Day 29

The worship of celestial controllers, the priest, guru and the wise; purity, honesty, celibacy, and non-violence—these are said to be the austerity of deed. (17.14)

Krishna told Arjun about three kinds austerities: of deed, word and thought. Austerity here does not mean self-denial, but an intelligent way of living in the right relationship with the material world, avoiding unnecessary wastage of energy.

To bow in respect before the gods, our teachers, the earth and its creatures and wise people is the right thing for us to do. It is considered as austerity of deed. To be pure inside out is also a part of austerity of deed. Internal cleaning happens by feeding the body right foods, and external cleaning by being strict about personal hygiene and cleanliness of surroundings.

To maintain the health of our physical body, apart from food and hygiene, right posture is also very important. Keeping the spine straight is a part of yoga. Body discipline is helpful in controlling the senses. Sense-control helps in curbing lust and non-violence, and focussing our attention on Self. All these good qualities constitute the austerity of deed.

Day 30

Speech that is non-offensive, truthful, pleasant, beneficial and uses regular references to scriptures is called the austerity of word. (17.15)

Speech is a powerful faculty, conveying words empowered by sound. It should be used carefully. One should not speak words that hurt or harm, or agitate the minds of others. Words once spoken cannot be taken back, they remain out there, penetrating the minds of listeners.

It is advised to only speak the truth, but avoid speaking it if it is hurtful to others. One has to be prudent in deciding whether, in any situation, being truthful is important or being quiet.

One should strive to engage in conversation that is both pleasant and beneficial to the listener, reflecting the wisdom of the scriptures. Talking too much should be avoided, as it turns into noise, as compared to measured talking which is like music to the ears.

Day 31

The serenity of mind, gentleness, silence, self-control, and the purity of thought; these are called the austerity of thought. (17.16)

Austerity of thought comprises five noble values. The first noble value is serenity of mind, which results from one's healthy relationship with the world. When our relationships are stress-free, our mind is also agitation-free.

The second value is gentleness, which allows only good and gentle thoughts to flow through the mind.

The third noble value is that of silence, which is not only not speaking or speaking less, but is an inward noiseless calm wherein no passions or desires are generated.

The fourth value is self-control, which is the ability to prevent our mind from constantly jumping from one thought to another.

The fifth value is purity of nature and honesty of motive, which means that the motivating thought behind any action should be noble.

NOVEMBER

Day 1

The above mentioned threefold austerity (of thought, word and deed) practised by yogis with supreme faith, without a desire for the fruit, is said to be in the mode of goodness. (17.17)

Anything, any service, any action, when performed selflessly, renouncing the fruits of action, is said to be sattvic or in the mode of goodness.

The goal of human life, the highest goal, is to connect to one's soul. When the threefold austerity of deed, word and thought is practised to attain this goal, it is termed sattvic.

When this threefold austerity is practised, not to gain anything except a better understanding of oneself, when it is practised with a balanced mind and with complete faith in its wisdom, it is done in the mode of goodness.

The threefold austerity is a great way to attain a sustained level of inner tranquillity, which makes it easy to achieve Self-realization.

Day 2

Austerity that is performed for gaining respect, honour, reverence and for the sake of show that yields an uncertain and temporary result, is said to be in the mode of passion. (17.18)

Anything, any service, any action, when performed with a selfish motive, is said to be rajasic or in the mode of passion. But a selfish motive need not always have a negative connotation. Selfish people think only for themselves, that is true. But that does not mean they are harming other people; it's just that they are not thinking about others.

When the threefold austerity of deed, word or thought is performed for worldly rewards, whether it is to gain other people's respect and admiration, or to win power and wealth for oneself, it is said to be in the mode of passion.

The hard-won rewards from such austerities are unstable and transitory. After all, in this fiercely competitive world of ours, whoever works the hardest gets rewarded. There are new winners all the time.

Day 3

Austerity performed with foolish stubbornness, or with self-torture, or for harming others, is declared to be in the mode of ignorance. (17.19)

Anything, any service, any action, when performed with foolish obstinacy, is said to be tamasic or in the mode of ignorance. When the threefold austerity includes bodily harm and self-torture, and that too with no clear thought about why it's being done, then it is considered tamasic.

Tamasic people are stubborn and pay no heed to any laws or reason. Their own reasoning is dead. They follow their foolish, unreasonable goals stubbornly, eventually causing harm to their own selves as well as others. They live in a perpetual state of rebellion.

The misconceived austerities, wrongly practised in the mode of ignorance, always bring about sorrow and discomfort.

Day 4

Charity that is given as a matter of duty, to a deserving candidate who does nothing in return, at the right place and time, is considered to be charity in the mode of goodness. (17.20)

Charity means giving. As with any action, charity also is of three kinds, sattvic, rajasic and tamasic.

A gift that is presented without any thought of receiving any compensation for it is a virtuous or sattvic gesture. Charity that is practised out of a sense of duty, to a deserving person, at the right time, with no strings attached, is considered to be charity in the mode of goodness.

At a physical level, to give food and money to a poor man is good; to give him a job is even better. To help him become well-qualified to obtain work is better still. On the mental level, educating an ignorant person is good, but training them to educate others is even better.

Day 5

Charity that is given unwillingly, or to get something in return, or looking for some fruit, is said to be in the mode of passion. (17.21)

Anything offered reluctantly is said to be rajasic or selfish. Charity that is given unwillingly, or with the hope of some kind of return, or some future reward, or as a repayment of past favours, is considered to be in the mode of passion. Such charities are not done with the emotion of 'giving'—they are done as a barter.

We find more people indulging in rajasic charity than sattvic these days. People feed the hungry on a particular day outside the temple of a particular god, with a very specific reason or request in their hearts.

Some people make a big show of donating money to charities, in order to garner respect from society, maybe even get an award or two in recognition of their service to humanity. These rajasic people are fooling themselves, not God.

Day 6

Charity that is given at a wrong place and time, and to unworthy persons, or without paying respect to the receiver, or with ridicule, is said to be in the mode of ignorance. (17.22)

Charity that humiliates the recipient, that which is unsuitable or is laced with contempt, or charity that is practised towards an unworthy person at an inappropriate time, is tamasic in nature.

Tamasic charity causes harm to both the receiver and the giver. One should not give money or gifts to evil people, as they would use that to do wrong things. Giving money to any person who indulges in intoxication or gambling would actually encourage that person to continue indulging in wrongful acts. This kind of charity, done in ignorance, would naturally be harmful to the giver, as he is the one helping the sinner to sin more.

When one offers help to another, with malice or insult, it arouses ill-will in the receiver. This act of charity is also tamasic.

Day 7

Aum Tat Sat is considered the threefold symbol of the all-pervading Spirit. Brahmins, the persons with divine qualities, the vedas, and the sacrificial rites were created by and from the Spirit. (17.23)

The unmanifested, the infinite, the changeless Spirit, is God or the universal energy. During the cycle of manifestation, the nameless and formless Spirit is described as Aum Tat Sat. It means: The Supreme is the Only Truth.

Aum is the creative vibration that upholds the world as prakriti. Tat is the intelligence that pervades the creation as the individual soul or purush. Sat is the father of all creation, the super-soul or Ishwar.

Humans display these three divine manifestations in themselves. Their body is the result of Aum. Their intelligence or Tat exists as their individual soul in the spiritual eye, between the eyebrows. Sat, the cosmic consciousness or super-soul, resides in their brain.

The eternal reality, Aum Tat Sat, is also the source of the vedas. Devotees who perform sacrificial rites listening to the holy sound of Aum Tat Sat soon attain cosmic perception and knowledge of the vedas. With the help of the vedas, they soon ascend to the cosmic consciousness and attain Self-realization, that is, they become brahmins or persons with divine (Brahm or God) qualities.

Day 8

Therefore, acts of sacrifice, charity and austerity prescribed in the scriptures are always commenced by uttering any one of the many names of God such as Aum, Amen, or Amin by the knowers of the Supreme. (17.24)

Krishna prescribes that any act of sacrifice, charity or austerity be preceded by chanting of Aum.

Aum of the vedas is the same as Hum of the Tibetans, Amin of the Muslims and Amen of the Christians and Jews. This sound is the voice of creation testifying the divine presence in everything.

When the holy syllable of Aum is chanted before any ritual, its vibrations cleanse any impurity that might be inadvertently present in the ritual. In fact, internalizing Aum and absorbing its vibration within, helps to cleanse our mind of restlessness and delusion.

Day 9

The seekers of salvation perform various types of sacrifice, charity and austerity by uttering 'He is all' without seeking a reward. (17.25)

After the devotee has merged with Aum, the next holy syllable is Tat. Chanting Tat, representing the cosmic intelligence, the devotee should perform selfless sacrifice or charity.

Salvation means liberation from physical, emotional and intellectual attachments. While performing any sacrifice, understanding the meaning of the term Tat as 'the universal oneness of the spiritual truth' is to work with no ego and consequent freedom from attachments. Once liberated, the devotee realizes the divinity in themselves.

The uttering of the word Tat also indicates that all the acts of sacrifice, penance and offerings by the devotee seeking atonement are undertaken without expecting any reward.

Day 10

The word 'truth' is used in the sense of Supreme Reality and the goodness emanating from it. The word 'truth' is also used for higher forms of spiritual action. (17.26)

After the devotees penetrate beyond Aum, the cosmic vibration, and Tat, the consciousness within all creation, they reach Sat, the Truth or God.

The good qualities and good activities of all human beings, demigods and liberated persons have their source in Sat, God the Father, the Absolute Truth. All the activities of the devotees by which they attain oneness with Cosmic Consciousness are Sat in nature. They are divine actions that lead to perception of God, the cosmic truth.

Day 11

Faith in sacrifice, charity and austerity is also called truth. The selfless service for the sake of the Supreme is verily termed as truth. (17.27)

The wise carry out their actions, offerings and charity with a faith that is steadfast and unwavering. This kind of faith is Sat. Selfless service, expecting nothing in return, is also Sat.

When the devotees have reached the ultimate state of soul realization, dissolving all restlessness by self-discipline and unwavering devotion, they merge with Sat, the Supreme Truth. In this process, the Tat also merges with Sat, and the illusion of duality disappears. This is the state of samadhi. The realm of finite creation and the infinity beyond are seen as one Cosmic Consciousness, the Absolute Reality—Sat.

Day 12

Whatever is done without faith, whether it is sacrifice, charity, austerity or any other act, is useless. It has no value here or hereafter. (17.28)

Spiritual practices that are done half-heartedly or carelessly are lacking in unconditional devotion and faith, hence considered Asat or against truth.

One who performs his devotional duties without any interest, finds his spiritual thirst to be unsatisfied in the current life. According to the karmic law, his spiritual thirst would remain unsatisfied in his next life and perhaps future lives too. He would never be able to break away from the cycle of rebirth.

Actions create consequences depending on the faith behind them. Krishna emphasizes that without faith evolution is not possible. Faithless actions would produce no results.

18

Final Revelation of the Ultimate Truth

13 November–31 December

Day 13

The sages define renunciation as abstaining from all work for personal profit. The wise define sacrifice as the sacrifice of, and the freedom from, the selfish attachment to the fruits of all work. (18.02)

Giving up of desire-prompted activities is renunciation, whereas giving up of fruits of action is relinquishment or sacrifice. Since desire is always for the fruit of action, renunciation and sacrifice seem similar in that respect. But there is a slight difference. Although both suggest giving up of desire, renunciation is giving up desire motivated action and sacrifice is giving up of desire for fruits of action. One is in the present frame, the other is in the future.

According to Krishna, work should be done after eliminating both the factors—desire prompted action and desire for its reward. In such a case, work becomes desireless action.

Day 14

Acts of selfless service, charity and austerity should not be abandoned, but should be performed, because selfless service, charity and austerity are the purifiers of the wise. (18.05)

Acts of selfless service, charity and austerity should never be given up, as these activities bring about a discipline in our body, mind and soul. Selfless service or sacrifice symbolizes performing the holy fire ceremony of casting the material desires into the fire of wisdom. The material desire then turns into longing for the divine.

Charity or giving can be turned around into giving to our own self. Charity begins at home, they say. Working on our own self, de-stressing and meditating would help us in following the right path to Self-realization. Austerities or self-disciplining activities are important to conquer physical restlessness, practise mental concentration, and strive for Self-realization.

Day 15

Even these obligatory works should be performed without attachment to the fruits. This is my definite advice. (18.06)

Like any other action, the acts of selfless service, charity and austerity, should also be performed without any sense of attachment. Attachment indicates presence of ego and its desires. Ego demands to be satisfied. Clinging to self-satisfaction limits the progress and delays attainment of absolute freedom of Spirit.

If any action is performed with attachment, the expectation of its fruits affect the efficiency of the action undertaken. To be rid of the anxiety for the fruits of the action, one has to get rid of attachment. This means renunciation of ego while performing action.

Day 16

Giving up one's duty is not proper. The abandonment of obligatory work is due to delusion and is declared to be in the mode of ignorance. (18.07)

Working for material satisfaction should be given up. But working towards spiritual evolution should never be given up. When a person renounces his engagement with good activities, he will find himself steeped in delusion, engaging in evil activities.

In a very gross example, we can see that children who do not spend some of their daily time in studying or pursuing any other intellectual activity, fall prey to spending their time in useless time-pass activities. Empty mind is the devil's workshop, we were told in school, and were encouraged to keep ourselves constructively occupied even during vacations.

Day 17

One who abandons duty merely because it is difficult or because of fear of bodily trouble, does not get the benefits of sacrifice by performing such a sacrifice in the mode of passion. (18.08)

A man quits his job and declares that he wants to do charity work. He feels that it was time he let go of the material world and help the needy. Sounds good. People praise him and his sacrifice. But there's a flip side to it.

The man was finding it increasingly difficult to cope up with the pressures of deadlines and targets in his workplace. He decided to quit before things got worse for him, and took on the option of charitable work. At his age, no other work was available to him.

His real story changed his sacrifice from sattvic to rajasic. He could fool his family and friends, but he could not fool himself and the God residing in him.

Day 18

Obligatory work performed as duty, renouncing selfish attachment to the fruit, is alone regarded to be sacrifice in the mode of goodness. (18.09)

Obligatory actions are divinely ordained duties. They include not only looking after our own selves, but also our family, neighbours and the country.

When a family member falls sick, we are duty-bound to help them. If there is a crisis at our neighbour's house, we should rush to offer our services. The basic duty of keeping our neighbourhood clean should be taken seriously by us. These are some of the things that we should do ungrudgingly, without expecting anything in return.

This kind of selfless service is regarded to be a sacrifice in the mode of goodness.

Day 19

The one who neither hates a disagreeable work, nor is attached to an agreeable work, is considered a renunciant, imbued with the mode of goodness and intelligence, and free from all doubts about the Supreme Being. (18.10)

True renunciants are sattvic by nature. They never hate any disagreeable work and environment, nor do they get attached to any agreeable field of action. They do their duties under all circumstances, without getting elated when successful or getting dejected when faced with obstacles. They are independent of the happenings around them and do not become victims of their own mental impressions.

Such people of equanimity are considered to be educated and cultured, with a clear vision of their goals. They know their field of activity, their own divine nature and their relationship with the world around them.

Day 20

Human beings cannot completely abstain from work. Therefore, the one who completely renounces the selfish attachment to the fruits of all work is considered a renunciant. (18.11)

Most of us are worldly people and perform most of our actions fulfilling the needs and desires of our own selves and our family.

A soul identified with the body may be said to be its slave. An embodied soul cannot relinquish its actions entirely. Those who know themselves as body rather than soul are a servant to the body. They have to work for it, during which they get entangled in the web of material desires.

The way out of this situation would be to completely renounce the attachment to the fruits of all work. By continuous meditation, we can disengage our mind from body consciousness and unite it with the consciousness of the soul. At this stage, we are able to renounce all desire for the fruits of action and perform our material duty with non-attachment of the soul.

Day 21

The threefold fruits of work—desirable, undesirable and mixed—accrue after death to the one who is not a renunciant, but never to a renunciant. (18.12)

As there are three modes of action, there are three modes of fruits of action too: desirable, undesirable and mixed.

Those who perform an action without renouncing its fruit, accrue the good, bad and mixed results of their three-fold karma. Every result deposits a seed tendency in the physical and astral brain of the person. At death, the sum total of the person's tendencies is stored in the individual soul of the person.

These stored up seeds, when watered by proper environment, sprout forth into specific results in this life and the next and so on. This is the theory of reincarnation.

The true relinquisher of the fruits of action, the renunciant, remains untouched by the three-fold actions. They are free.

Day 22

Sankhya doctrine describes five factors for the accomplishment of all actions. They are: the physical body, the seat of karma; the ego, the doer; the organs of perception and action, the instruments; the various bio-impulses; and the fifth is the presiding deities of the organs. (18.13–18.14)

Sankhya, the highest wisdom, is to have complete knowledge or ultimate enlightenment. According to Krishna, there are five aspects of action laid out in the Sankhya philosophy.

The first is the physical body or the gateway for the entrance of the stimuli. It is the place of all physical, mental and spiritual actions. The second is the ego that seeks fulfilment of the actions through the body. It is the performer or doer of actions.

The third aspect is the organs of perception and action along with their coordinator, the mind. These are the instruments through which the individual soul comes into contact with the field of enjoyment. The fourth aspect is the bio-impulses generated in the body by the organs of perception and action.

The fifth aspect is the self-created destiny of the person. It comprises the effects of past actions, which function as ruling tendencies (deities), having a compelling influence in the person's present and future actions.

Day 23

Whatever action, whether right or wrong, one performs by thought, word and deed; these are its five causes. (18.15)

The five aspects listed in the Sankhya philosophy are the causative factors behind all actions, right or wrong. Right action here means action in accordance to the principles prescribed in the scriptures, and wrong actions are those that are against the prescribed principles.

All actions that we do, through thought, word or deed, cannot happen without our body as their happening place, their stage. Neither can we perform any actions without our limbs and our sense organs as the instruments of performance. Our mind has an important role to play too; it processes everything that the sense organs sense and then decides what action to take. With everything in place, we need the energy to act, which is provided by our life-force.

Finally, fate comes into the picture. It is our own past karmic baggage that pushes us in a certain direction, making us choose one action over another.

Day 24

The ignorant one who considers one's body or soul as the sole doer due to imperfect knowledge, does not understand. (18.16)

According to Krishna, a person of little understanding or great arrogance would believe that they are the doers of all their actions. But then, most people are like that.

An artist sees the brush in his hands, colours on the palette and the painting on the easel he is working on, and says, 'I am painting.' That is his reality. Even in the simplest of tasks, like walking or eating, the doer seems to be the one who is physically doing. According to Krishna, this is ignorance.

Coming events cast their shadows long before, is a popular saying. It means that talent cannot be hidden for long. If we look around, we'll see that children do not necessarily follow their parents' professions. Why? The children may have the genes from their parents for their physical features, but that's all. What their mental inclinations or tendencies are, are based on their karmic baggage from their own past.

When we encounter an immensely talented singer in a family of non-singers, we call him a prodigy, and his talent as god-gift. It is nothing of that sort. The singer is just finishing off where he left from in his past life.

Day 25

The one who is free from the notion of doership, and whose intellect is not polluted by the desire to reap the fruit, even after slaying people, he or she neither slays, nor is bound by the act of killing. (18.17)

People who understand the five doers, and know that none of those five is the real them, and carry on their duties diligently, without desire or anxiety, with a calm mind, would not be bound by their actions. Even if such people kill their enemies, they have not really committed a crime.

Here, Krishna emphasizes to Arjun that even if he killed his kith and kin in the war, he would not be doing anything wrong. This was a kind of concluding statement from Krishna in response to Arjun's original dilemma.

The essence was that if a person frees themselves from ego and identification with their body, they would renounce all actions as they were brought about by ignorance of the true nature of Self. Such a person would then remain unaffected by the fruits of their actions.

Day 26

The knowledge, the known and the knower are the threefold driving force to an action. The 11 organs, the act, and the agent or the modes of material nature, are the three components of action. (18.18)

What makes one act? First is the object, which is perceived by our sense organs and interpreted by our mind. This is called 'knowledge'.

Second is our own understanding about the object, based on what we have heard, seen or experienced in the past, which makes us love it, hate it, or be indifferent to it. This is called 'known'. Third, depending on our own feelings towards the object, we either choose to pursue it, reject it or do nothing. This is called 'knower'.

So, even with the five causes or doers of action that were discussed earlier, we still need this three-fold driving force of knowledge, known and knower, to make an action happen.

Day 27

The knowledge by which one sees a single immutable reality in all beings as undivided in the divided, is in the mode of goodness. (18.20)

We have seen the three modes of nature being reflected in doers and their actions. We can also see that all doers understand an object based on their own past experiences or their own limited knowledge, and react differently to it. Hence, knowledge also can be divided into three types: sattvic, rajasic and tamasic.

Some people understand that even though there appears to be an infinite variety of creatures and objects in the world, there is an underlying unity in their diversity. Such people do not differentiate between creatures, as they see beyond the external appearances, the divine essence or one life that is in all of them. This is right understanding; this mode of knowledge is said to be sattvic.

Day 28

The knowledge by which one sees different realities of various types among all beings as separate from one another, is considered to be in the mode of passion. (18.21)

The concept that the material body is the living entity and that, with the destruction of the body the consciousness is also destroyed, is called knowledge in the mode of passion or rajasic knowledge. It believes in the plurality of the world.

According to this, people see the different creatures and objects in the world to be different and separate from each other, and separate from themselves. These people consider some creatures worthy of admiration and others worthy only of disgust. They love some objects and hate others.

Rajasic knowledge is superficial and delusive. Based on delusive knowledge, some people consider themselves to be superior to others, based on which they mistreat them.

Day 29

The irrational, baseless and worthless knowledge by which one clings to one single effect (such as the body) as if it is everything, is declared to be in the mode of darkness of ignorance (18.22)

There are some who see only what they want to see and believe that what they see is the only thing that matters. They cling blindly to their narrow view and do not see the rest of the world at all, or listen to any other opinion. This is tamasic knowledge.

People of tamasic understanding thoughtlessly engage in trivial aspirations, those they think will cause them the least trouble and give the maximum pleasure. Physical, bodily satisfaction is their ultimate goal in life. They never question the correctness of their motives, as their befuddled understanding justifies all their personal convictions, however contrary to the principles of truth they might be.

Tamasic perception views the body and the need to satisfy its demands as the sole reason for existence.

Day 30

The obligatory duty performed without likes and dislikes, and without selfish motives and attachment to enjoy the fruit, is said to be in the mode of goodness. (18.23)

Our actions are as said also divided into three types: sattvic, rajasic and tamasic. Sattvic actions are those that are one's own obligatory duties towards society, performed without any attachments to the fruits thereof. These actions are not motivated by likes and dislikes—they are just performed spontaneously.

Such actions are undertaken by people who possess sattvic knowledge. They seek fulfilment and joy in all the work they do; for them, work is worship. A sattvic action produces peace and harmony in society.

If people do charitable work to help the needy, where the needy are genuinely benefitting, then their action would be called sattvic. But if the person is doing charity for the purpose of gaining publicity for himself, then the sattvic action becomes rajasic.

DECEMBER

Day 1

Action performed with ego, with selfish motives and with too much effort, is declared to be in the mode of passion. (18.24)

Rajasic action comes from rajasic knowledge. Such action is undertaken to satisfy one's desire in a spirit of arrogance, egoism and vanity. Most people indulge in this category of action. They are engaged in mundane pursuits, motivated by self-interest and worldly desires. Their actions express an urgency to keep up with the standards of the day, with an emphasis on material wealth.

Passionate people, concerned only with their own selves, perform work that they dislike with reluctance, resisting and complaining. At the same time, when it comes to work that they like or that which brings them some gain, they do it with much eagerness. Desire-based rajasic actions generate more desires and result in a continuous cycle of rebirths.

Day 2

Action that is undertaken because of delusion, disregarding consequences, loss, injury to others, as well as one's own ability, is said to be in the mode of ignorance. (18.25)

Tamas is the dark quality that affects the knowledge of human beings; their actions too, reflect their ignorance.

People who act thoughtlessly under the influence of violent emotions, not concerned with the consequences of their actions, not only hurt others but hurt themselves too. Due to their irrational behaviour, tamasic people entangle themselves and their loved ones in all kinds of difficulties.

Tamasic action is characterized by inertia. It always pursues the path of least resistance to avoid the effort required in the practice of self-control and exercise of discrimination.

Day 3

The doer who is free from attachment, is non-egotistic, endowed with resolve and enthusiasm and unperturbed in success or failure, is called good. (18.26)

Those people, whose minds are not bound by the ego or attached to material things, who perform divinely motivated actions that help others, disregarding success or failure, are sattvic doers. Such people are able to distinguish temporal mortal dreams from the eternal reality, hence they are totally free from attachments. Sattvic doers remain unperturbed with their success or failure. In fact, they don't see themselves as doers at all; they believe God to be working through them.

Though it may seem highly improbable, but good sattvic workers do exist in the material world. They are happy in their workplace, as they do not recognize any competition and are focussed in their work. At home too, such people remain calm in any stressful situation, which helps the other family members also to relax. They diligently perform their duties, whether at home or at the workplace, without any expectations. Such people are a blessing to have around.

Day 4

The doer who is impassioned, attached to the fruits of their work, greedy, violent, impure and is affected by joy and sorrow, is called passionate. (18.27)

The person who is under the influence of passionate energy is said to be rajasic in nature. Always restless and outgoing, a rajasic person is completely materialistic, blindly amassing money, property and other material goods with immense greed and self-interest.

Rajasic people can be insensitive, harsh, sadistic, revengeful, ready to hurt or destroy any competitor or anyone standing in their way of self-interest. They are greedy, thinking that whatever they have amassed is permanent. They are happy when they are successful, but much distressed and angry when not.

The sole aim of life of rajasic people is to make this world as materially comfortable as possible for themselves.

Day 5

The undisciplined, vulgar, stubborn, wicked, malicious, lazy, depressed, and procrastinating doer is called ignorant. (18.28)

More often than not, the doers who are not successful in life have a tamasic nature. They blame everyone else, except their own selves, for their miseries. They never find fault with their own inherent laziness, their own nature of procrastination and indiscipline.

Like a butterfly, a tamasic doer's mind and body are forever restless. Lacking the intelligence for decisiveness and the will for constructive action, such people are pulled in one direction and then the other by any momentary influence. These people are morally crude and vulgar, indulging in evil actions whenever the impulse arises in them. Tamasic people can unscrupulously deceive others, behaving like Dr Jekyll and Mr Hyde.

Day 6

The intellect by which one understands the path of work and the path of renunciation, right and wrong action, fear and fearlessness, bondage and liberation, that intellect is in the mode of goodness. (18.30)

Our intellect also has three modes: sattvic, rajasic and tamasic. When the intellect is unclouded and is in a mode of goodness, the consciousness rises to manifest as intuition. This makes the person instinctively understand, in any circumstance, what should be done and what shouldn't be.

Sattvic discrimination in people reveals to them the bondage of pursuing worldly activities. It shows how the path of self-satisfaction is endless and makes a person constantly apprehensive about failure and death.

A sattvic intellect is intuitively perceptive, fearless, steadfast and calm. And because it is free from any material attachments, it leads the person through life's ups and downs with ease.

Day 7

The intellect by which one cannot distinguish between righteousness (dharma) and unrighteousness (adharma) and right and wrong action is in the mode of passion. (18.31)

The mode of passion clouds the intellect. Such people are not always sure what is right and what is wrong. They are confused because their only concern is how any action affects them.

A rajasic intellect makes people hold on strongly to things that give them pleasure, power and wealth. Blindly following sensual pursuits, such people soon get trapped in a web of worries and disillusionment. Since rajasic intellect inherently lacks trust, it leads such people from pillar to post. Unfortunately, happiness always eludes them. Such people are never satisfied with anything in life.

Day 8

The intellect, when covered by ignorance, accepts unrighteousness (adharma) as righteousness (dharma), and thinks everything to be that which it is not, is in the mode of ignorance. (18.32)

Tamasic intellect is dark with ignorance. Such people are convinced about the rightness of wrongdoing. They see things from a twisted, perverted point of view. All actions emerging out of a tamasic intellect lead to misery. And since a tamasic person cannot think coherently, they indulge in more evil actions.

Such people have an extremist mentality and overindulge in sensual pleasures like eating, sex, getting inebriated, gambling and so on. They are irresponsible towards themselves as well as others and lead an unnatural existence. Such abnormal people are a danger to themselves and the society they live in.

Day 9

The resolve by which one manipulates the functions of the mind, prana (bio-impulses) and senses, for God-realization alone, is in the mode of goodness. (18.33)

Fortitude or resolve is of three kinds: sattvic, rajasic and tamasic. Fortitude is defined as a combination of courage and patience. It is the consistency of purpose and self-application with which a person pursues his goal. Our intellect decides our goal as well as chooses the path for us to follow to achieve it without getting distracted.

Our fortitude makes us stick to it.

The resolve with which one steadily controls one's mind, sense organs and their activities, maintaining an unwavering focus on the goal, is considered to be in the mode of goodness.

Sattvic fortitude makes a person see God in everything. Such people are helped by their own intuitive sense of discrimination, which steers them away from evil people and evil actions. A person with sattvic fortitude can wander in the worldly life, engaging in dutiful activities, beholding good and evil, without getting affected or entangled in them.

Day 10

The resolve by which a person, craving for the fruits of work, clings to duty, accumulating wealth and enjoyment with great attachment, is in the mode of passion. (18.34)

When a person's inner patience is influenced by worldly attachments, it is said to be in the mode of passion. Such a person holds on firmly to actions that give him wealth, power and sensual pleasure.

People who are always looking for their own benefit in the religious or economic activities that they engage in, whose only desire is sense gratification, are in the mode of passion or rajas.

People with rajasic disposition keep their mind and senses patiently and persistently settled in worldly tasks. Most people belong to this category and we see them focussed on earning money, maintaining a family and superficially participating in religious ceremonies.

Day 11

The resolve by which a dull person does not give up sleep, fear, grief, despair and carelessness, is in the mode of ignorance. (18.35)

Those who cannot avoid oversleeping, who cannot avoid the pride of enjoying the material world, in fact whose mind and senses are always engaged in dreaming of lording over the material world, are said to be in the mode of ignorance. This tamasic quality makes the person obstinately cling to evil.

Oversleeping results in mental and physical indolence and aversion to constructive work. Lack of activity produces dejection through the consciousness of a useless existence. After all, in our heart we know our own reality. Ultimately, this low-spiritedness gives rise to grief and hopelessness.

Unfortunately, the inherent contempt of tamasic people towards the need to change keeps them away from any hope of salvation and they remain in a state of unhappy existence.

Day 12

The pleasure that appears as poison in the beginning, but is like nectar in the end, comes by the grace of Self-knowledge, and is in the mode of goodness. (18.37)

Everyone wants to be happy. Happiness is the universal aim of life. But then, we all have our own definitions of happiness. Violence makes a tamasic person happy, whereas wealth and power make a rajasic person happy. To a person sattvic at heart, the pleasure of self-control leading to self-perfection is unmatched to any other sensual happiness.

Initially, the person may go through stages of struggle, when they are trying to control their senses. But once they are under control, the person feels a blissful sense of freedom. His soul becomes free. This happiness is permanent because it becomes a state of being. The pleasure of Self-knowledge, therefore, is considered to be in the mode of goodness.

Day 13

Sensual pleasures appear as nectar in the beginning, but become poison in the end, and are in the mode of passion. (18.38)

People work hard, save money and then buy a car or a house, thinking that it's an achievement of sorts to buy those things. They expect to be happy on having achieved their goal. And they are happy for a while, till their possessions or achievements start giving them trouble. A house needs regular maintenance, so does a car. Then these very possessions become troublesome; those that were the cause of pleasure become the cause of pain.

This mode of happiness, which is governed by passion, is considered to be rajasic. It is temporary happiness, as it is dependent on the material object. Any pleasure derived from the combination of senses and sense objects eventually results in distress.

Worldly people or rajasic people, young or old, are those who overindulge their senses. Even after discovering the harmful after-effects, they are still helplessly driven towards excesses. Why? Because these people are trapped in the web of their own bad habits.

Day 14

Pleasure that confuses a person in the beginning and in the end; which comes from sleep, laziness and carelessness, is said to be in the mode of ignorance. (18.39)

We have heard from our grandparents that if we sleep too much, our mind also falls asleep. It is true. Too much sleep paralyses the mental faculties of people; they lose any sense of discrimination. So the pleasure derived from sleep and laziness is certainly in the mode of darkness or ignorance.

Such tamasic people live in a constant state of illusion. They are happy living in the belief that not doing anything is the best thing in the world. Anything that lies unused for some time becomes useless.

So is the case with these people. Ultimately, they start losing the use of their own arms and legs.

Tamasic people may believe that they are leading a royal life, but once they become physically and mentally useless, even their own people start shunning them. This, truly, is a mode of ignorance.

Day 15

There is no being, either on the earth or among the celestial controllers in heaven, who can remain free from these three modes of material nature. (18.40)

Krishna says that there is no creature either on the earth or among the gods in heaven who is free from the influences of the three modes of nature: sattva, rajas and tamas. The interplay of these modes is the very expression of nature. It is the varying combination of these modes that makes us all so different.

Even though both humans and gods have the power of choosing how they want to behave or what they want to do and be responsible for their actions, yet they cannot escape the influence of these three modes which are endemic in nature.

The entire fabric of manifestation is held together by the interweaving threads of the three modes of nature. We cannot escape it. But we can surely use our intellect and refuse to succumb to the temptations, and transcend these modes to merge with the source, or God.

Day 16

The division of human labour is also based on the qualities inherent in peoples' nature or their make-up. (18.41)

With the three measuring parameters, Krishna classified the entire humanity under four distinct types. The classification is based on the inner qualities of people, their basic nature that guides them to do whatever they do best in life. These qualities are inherent in a person and have nothing to do with having been born in a particular family. In fact, they are more to do with the person's karmic past.

According to Krishna, there are four types of people: brahmins, kshatriyas, vaishyas and shudras. Their difference is due to the difference in the level of sattva, rajas and tamas in their nature.

When a person manifests predominantly the good sattva qualities, then they are considered a brahmin, or one who knows the Self. When a person has a mix of good sattvic qualities and rajasic passion, and is constantly striving to control their senses, then they are considered a kshatriya, or a warrior. When a person manifests predominantly the rajasic passion, tempered a little with the ignorance of tamas, then they are considered a vaishya, a worldly person. One who has predominantly tamasic qualities is considered a shudra or a body-identified person.

Day 17

Those who have serenity, self-control, purity, patience, honesty, transcendental knowledge and belief in God are labelled as intellectuals or brahmins. Those having the qualities of heroism, vigour, firmness, dexterity, not fleeing from battle, charity and administrative skills are called leaders or protectors or kshatriyas. (18.42–18.43)

They who have realized oneness with the universal energy or God have no trace of any delusion in their consciousness. Such people possess great self-control and tolerance. They are pure and upright in action, thought and word; they are wise and follow the teachings of scriptures, even if they have not read them. Their nature is dominated by sattva and they are considered as brahmins.

They who are heroic in the face of adversity, a courageous fighter in the face of injustice, and generous to those who follow them, they are resourceful and dependable leaders who never turn their back on a righteous battle, or a mission they have undertaken. Their nature is dominated by rajas with a smattering of sattva, and they are considered to be kshatriyas. Such people constantly fight to control their senses.

Day 18

Those who are good in cultivation, cattle-breeding, business, trade, finance and industry are known as businessmen or vaishyas. Those who are good in service to others, in all types of menial work, are known as workers or shudras. (18.44)

A person who is involved in keeping the wheels of trade and agriculture moving, creating wealth so that society's needs are fulfilled, is known as a vaishya. They are businesspeople or traders. A vaishya garners wisdom from the sages and uses it to improve his life. And by exemplifying their own life, they offer that knowledge to others. They take from one, work on it and give it to another—this is typically a vaishya activity.

A person who is happy to serve others is a shudra. They are diligent and loyal in the performance of their duty, content to follow orders and instructions, and to carry them out to the best of their ability. Body-bound people, who are busy only in earning money to support their bodily needs, and who prefer to sleep when they are not labouring, are typically shudras.

Day 19

One attains perfection by worshipping the Supreme Being—from whom all beings originate, and by whom this entire universe is pervaded—through performance of one's natural duty for Him. (18.46)

We have learnt this by now that it's our own karmic baggage that determines our present birth. We have to reap what we have sowed in our past. The liberation from this bondage is through working out the effects by performing our present duties selflessly. If we don't, we would carry the karmic baggage on to the next life.

To liberate ourselves from the present bondage, the first step is that we must understand that wherever we are born, the family, the circumstances, all are because of our own past karma. We need to accept this fact first, make peace with it and never complain about it.

The second step is that we should work hard selflessly, for that is the only way we would be able to look after ourselves and our basic needs. Selfless working would entail that while working we are not thinking of ourselves, but are thinking of how our work is helping others. This would free us from all the work-related stress as well. When we believe in 'work is worship', we unconsciously serve God by serving others. This is the path to Self-realization.

Day 20

One's inferior natural work is better than superior unnatural work even though well-performed. One who does the work ordained by one's inherent nature, without any selfish motive, incurs no sin or karmic reaction. (18.47)

According to Krishna, if we are sincerely following our duty in work, then we do not incur any karmic reaction. Simply put, we incur no sin. If a soldier kills enemies in a war, it is not considered a sin, as it's a part of his duties. A criminal lawyer defends his client, wins the case, and his criminal client is set free. It may seem wrong to us, but the lawyer did his duty. If there seems to be any injustice, the onus falls on the judge or the judicial system, but not the lawyer.

Another important thing that comes to light here is that we must follow our 'calling'. Every person has a 'calling', which is the path ordained for them to clear their past karmic debts. This is how the soul evolves. The problem is that we choose to ignore the call of our soul. We follow the path that others choose for us, be it our parents, teachers or peers.

It is seen many times that people, after having studied engineering or medicine, after having worked in multi-national organizations, suddenly leave everything one day and get involved in charitable work. Why? Because they finally hear the call of their soul. It's not surprising that doing the latter makes them happier than their high-paying jobs.

Day 21

Endowed with purified intellect, subduing the mind with firm resolve, turning away from the objects of the senses, giving up likes and dislikes, living in solitude, eating lightly, controlling the mind, speech and organs of action, ever absorbed in yoga of meditation and taking refuge in detachment; and after relinquishing egotism, violence, pride, lust, anger, and proprietorship one becomes peaceful, free from the notion of 'I, me and mine', and fit for attaining oneness with the Supreme Being. (18.51–18.53)

Those whose intellect is free from all sensual entanglements, keep themselves in the mode of goodness. Such people are the controllers of their own minds and keep their perception focussed on Self. They abandon the luxuries of their senses, beginning with the desire to hear and be heard. Free of likes and dislikes, such a person is satisfied with the bare necessities for sustaining life.

Eating lightly is indicative of eating just enough to sustain the body. Living in solitude does not necessarily mean living alone, but rather living a detached life. When one is detached from the material world, one becomes calm inside; it's like being an island in the middle of a choppy ocean.

Those people who can disconnect their minds from all distractions and attractions, who are free from desires and attachments, who are free from the consciousness of 'I, me and mine'—such people are fit to merge with the source, the universal energy or the Supreme Being.

Day 22

Absorbed in the Supreme Being, the serene one neither grieves, nor desires; becoming impartial to all beings, one obtains the highest devotional love for God. (18.54)

It is our ego that creates a divide between us and the others. It makes us judge everyone all the time. It makes us evaluate everything on a material scale. It fans our desires to acquire more and more material possessions. Simply put, it binds us down inextricably to the material world.

After eliminating egotism and its manifestations in the form of power, pride, lust and sense of possession, the devotee experiences tremendous peace within, as they become free from all false evaluations of life.

Such people become detached and desireless; they become impartial to all as they see God in all beings. When such a person becomes one with the Self, they also becomes the seer, like the Self, like God.

Day 23

By devotion one truly understands what and who I am in essence. Having known me in essence, one immediately merges with me. (18.55)

In order to understand or know someone or something, we need to devote our full attention to it. That devotion makes us a devotee. The same principle applies to understanding the universal energy or God. We need to devote our complete undistracted attention to him. Once we do that, then like any other subject or object, we would have a clear understanding of him.

We would then understand that the universal energy or God is devoid of all forms and names. The various forms and names are those of the universal energy manifested as nature.

Knowing God as non-dual, unborn, unchanging and undying

consciousness is also the same as knowing one's own Self. Once it is clear that it is the same energy that pervades the entire universe including us, it is also clear that we all are one. That is meant by merging in God.

Day 24

A karma yogi devotee attains the eternal immutable abode by my grace, even while doing all duties, just by taking refuge in me, by surrendering all actions to me with loving devotion. (18.56)

We are taught from childhood to have a goal to follow. All our adult life too, is spent on following some goal or the other. Even a ship sailing on the high seas is going from one port to another. A river has its goal—the ocean it merges into. Likewise, every being born has a goal too, and it is not to die, but to merge with its source.

It follows that if we just work selflessly without desiring the fruits of our action, we would succeed in getting rid of our past karmic debts. We would even find a place in heaven. But we would not be able to merge with the Supreme or universal energy. Why? The answer is simple. We never made it as our goal to achieve. We made selfless work as our goal.

In order to merge with our creator, the Supreme, we need to make him our goal. So, while doing our selfless work, we need to constantly think of God, surrendering all our actions to him. This would make us achieve our goal of Self or God realization.

Day 25

Sincerely offer all actions to me, set me as your supreme goal and completely depend on me. Always fix your mind on me, and resort to karma yoga. (18.57)

Krishna tells Arjun to disconnect his ego from his mind and the sense of doership of actions, and unite his intellect with God, feeling him as the doer of all actions.

When in the performance of any action, a person's mind is identified with the ego, it becomes bound in the sense experiences and material activities. Such people, whether they want it or not, experience the emotions of like-dislike, love-hate and so on.

But when the person's mind is identified with God, it ceases to get entangled in the sensual experiences of like-dislike, etc., because in such a case the ego does not exist. With no ego to pacify or pamper, the person becomes free. Such an unfettered person, focusing on God while performing any action, is on the right path.

Day 26

You are controlled by your own nature-born karmic impressions. Therefore, you shall do, even against your will, what you do not wish to do out of delusion. (18.60)

Krishna tells Arjun that if he felt that fighting was wrong or if he was under any illusion that he could escape from participating in it, then he was wrong. Being born as a warrior, Arjun's basic nature was to fight against injustice, to fight for the cause of righteousness. It was not possible for him to escape from his mode of nature. His own rajasic nature would compel Arjun to fight. This is the law of nature.

The advice here is that we should perform our duty neither unwillingly, nor with attachment, but with the objective of liberating ourselves from the bondage of the material world.

I would go a step further and say that following the call of our soul is very important, as it is that which guides us on the right path, the path ordained for us by our own mode of nature.

Day 27

The Supreme Lord, as the controller abiding in the inner psyche of all beings, causes them to work out their karma, like a puppet mounted on a machine. (18.61)

The Supreme Lord or the universal energy pervades all beings as super-soul. We know by now that we are a combination of body, individual soul and super-soul. The individual soul carries the karmic impressions from our past and we live and function according to that. Super-soul is the observer.

After the death of the physical body, the individual soul moves on to another body to carry out the leftover karma. All beings are, therefore, being governed by their own karmic impressions. They go on living and dying, mechanically moving along the cycles of rebirth.

All this action happens because the Supreme Lord created the universe and manifested all the beings. Since he is the super-soul, his energy is manifested as the individual soul as well as our body. He is the ultimate controller of the entire show.

Day 28

Renounce all dharma of body, mind and intellect, and just surrender completely to my will with firm faith and loving devotion. I shall liberate you from all sins and the bonds of karma. (18.66)

People live with all kinds of perceived attachments and duties towards their own body, mind and intellect and exist as individuals. That individuality expresses itself as their ego. These perceived duties do not constitute the real dharma of a person.

The real dharma of a living being is to merge with the source. Keeping this in mind, the perceived dharma should be renounced. Renouncing would mean that we should not allow ourselves to identify again and again with our ego and the entrapments that accompany it.

A single-pointed steady contemplation of the Self, that is God, would help in withdrawing from the sensory material world. It would also liberate us from our sins, which are the agitations of our mind. A calm mind devoted to Self merges with Self and frees us from the karmic cycle.

Day 29

Whoever shall impart to my devotees the transcendental knowledge of the Gita, shall be performing the highest devotional service to me, and shall certainly come to me. (18.68–18.69)

This is a commandment that not only one should study the Gita but must also pass on the benefit of such knowledge to others in society. The idea is that if the knowledge is not transferred from one person to another, there would not be any mobility of intelligence. It is not necessary that one has to first become a master of the entire Gita. The purpose is to spread knowledge, however much we have learnt and imbibed.

God is conscious of his creation, he is aware of the sufferings that many people go through. So, any person who does the job of helping people understand their innate divinity, helps them to alleviate their suffering. Such a person who leads others to liberation, is naturally loved by God the most.

Day 30

Arjun: Destroyed is my delusion as I have gained my memory through your grace. I stand firm with my doubts dispelled. I shall act according to your word. (18.73)

Arjun admits that his confusions have ended and that he has woken up from his state of unconsciousness. This statement is not just a meek acceptance; it is an affirmation of Arjun recognizing his real nature.

Arjun wakes up from his dream-state where he had identified

with his ego, like all of us do. His doubts were destroyed and his delusions had disappeared. His mind was now clear of all conflict and he was ready to perform his duty to the best of his abilities. With full faith in his dear friend and charioteer Krishna, Arjun the warrior, was ready to fight for righteousness.

It is important not just to hear or read a lecture, but also to see its impact on people, see how it changes a person's life completely. After all, we all learn by seeing examples that we can identify with. Identifying with Krishna may not be easy, but identifying with Arjun is a piece of cake!

Day 31

Sanjay: Wherever there will be Krishna, the Lord of Yoga, and Arjun, a true devotee, wielding the weapon of self-control, there will be everlasting prosperity, victory, welfare and morality. (18.78)

In this concluding verse, Sanjay, after witnessing the enlightenment of Arjun, declares that whoever becomes like Arjun, who, though weak initially, was still ready to free himself by slaying his would-be captors, his senses, with the bow of self-control, and who was able to unite his soul with the super-soul—such a person is bound to find everlasting happiness.

By practising non-attachment and by withdrawal of consciousness from sense perceptions with the help of yoga and meditation, a person can unite his soul with the Spirit and attain eternal peace and happiness. And this is the aim of all living beings.

Acknowledgments

Writing this book has been a beautiful journey of introspection and learning.

I must start by thanking Avdhesh, my husband, who made me relocate to the hills of Uttarakhand, my home state, to write. He understood my need to internalize the Gita first before spilling it out on paper.

I have Kapish Mehra to thank for, for nudging me into taking this journey inwards, the result of which is here for you to read. This is my second book with him, the first one being on Krishna's management skills. Hopefully, between Rupa and myself, there would be many more 'gods' to write about.

Thank you dear Rudra, you are the best commissioning editor I have met so far. It's people like you who seed the author into giving their best.